STORM
OF THE
CENTURY

New England's
Great Blizzard of 1978

Christopher J. Haraden

T I M E S
SQUARE
B O O K S
Hanover, Massachusetts

Copyright ©2003 Christopher J. Haraden

Printed and bound in the United States of America

Times Square Books is an imprint of Times Square Media Corporation.

Visit us on the World Wide Web: www.timessquarebooks.com
e-mail: info@timessquarebooks.com

First printing 2003

ISBN: 0-9727845-0-0
Library of Congress Control Number: 2002096940

Quantity discounts are available on bulk purchases of this book for reselling, educational purposes, subscription incentives, gifts or fund-raising. Special books, booklets or book excerpts can also be created to fit specific needs. For information, contact the publisher: Times Square Books, 30 Aspen Drive, Hanover, MA 02339, 781-982-1517, e-mail: info@timessquarebooks.com.

Cover photo credits:
Front, clockwise from top left: National Archives and Records Administration; Stanley Bauman; U.S. Army Corps of Engineers; Kevin Cole/Boston Herald.
Back: National Archives and Records Administration.

*This book is dedicated to
my wife, Marilyn,
and our son, Matthew.
Both of you inspire me every day.*

"Soon the storm will be romance for most of us, memories recalled to break the humdrum. In the press of getting back to work, or recovering from the costly leisure of lost days, we may forget the common sense the storm forced upon us. We may forget about the necessity to prepare for the next storm.

"Perhaps more dangerous, we may forget how vulnerable to nature we are and will remain, no matter what our preparation."
— Editorial, The Boston Globe, Feb. 12, 1978

"I could speak volumes about the inhuman perversity of the New England weather."
— Mark Twain, in a speech to the
New England Society, Dec. 22, 1876

Table of Contents

Acknowlegments

One author's name appears on the cover of this book, but many people assisted in its creation.

Apologies in advance to anyone whose name is inadvertently omitted.

Thanks a 'Hullava lot' (see Chapter 6) to:

Susan Ovans, for her editing expertise, Barry J. Haraden, Michael S. Dukakis, Elaine M. Zeman, Frank Florianz, Stanley Bauman, Kevin Cole and Arthur Pollack, M. Frances Keyes, Nazzareno DiVito, Jr., Bruce Simons, Rosalyn Glikin Simons, John Galluzzo, Dan Johnson, Myron Klayman, Norman Rogers, Guy Rizzo, Timothy Hays of the U.S. Army Corps of Engineers, Paul Palermo of the National Archives and Records Administration, Joan L. Gearin of the National Archives and Records Administration, Maureen Aldrich of the Providence Journal, Linda Henderson of the Providence Journal, James Plugh of The Patriot Ledger, Linda Chapman of The Patriot Ledger, the Hull Lifesaving Museum, The Board of Trustees of the Fort Revere Park & Preservation Society, and last, and certainly not least, my wife, Marilyn Haraden.

Prologue

"Slowly, it began to be understood – while the blizzard stood still and raged – that it was the little towns on the Massachusetts shores that had suffered the most. The discomfort of the big cities was nothing compared to what such coastal areas endured.

"The wind and water scythed through the towns. Houses were tossed about like toys. Cars were buried in the mud. Boats were shoved into living rooms. People feared for their lives while every-thing else they owned was taken by the sea.

"It was like a whirlwind in a toothpick factory. Suddenly, the 27 inches of snow in Boston and up to 40 inches in Rhode Island seemed of little consequence. Snow can be moved. It requires only time and money.

"There were too many things to put it all in focus at once. Black-outs affecting 100,000 Bostonians; jammed freeways everywhere; avaricious looters; a mounting death toll; exhausted, stranded people; and in Hull, people peered out under their first blue skies in three days to view streets filled with water, houses torn to shreds and mud and debris everywhere."

United Press International storm update, Feb. 12, 1978

I weathered the Great Blizzard of 1978 huddled with my family in front of our fireplace on the side of a hill in Hull, Massachusetts, listening to a battery-powered radio and playing board games by lantern light.

As the wind howled through the night, the radio crackled with weather reports, evacuation instructions and updates on where people could take shelter. On one station, the hosts tried to lighten the mood by recycling the beach and boating reports from a previous summer's heat wave.

On another station, listeners telephoned to detail storm conditions from their corner of the state. We heard pleas for help from one frequent caller, a fellow Hull resident, stranded with his family at his flooded home in the low-lying part of town. With each call, his situation became more urgent – the water was rising quickly, the power was out, the wind and snow were blowing hard. Rescuers in an amphibious vehicle eventually brought them to a shelter, where they joined hundreds of others – like my wife, Marilyn, and her family – who had been marooned by the rising tides or were trapped in homes without heat.

That caller's plight underscored the helplessness that even rescue workers faced during the blizzard. We would learn later that firefighters in our town and in other communities were forced to let houses burn because they simply couldn't reach them. How ironic that an overabundance of snow and water would impede the fire trucks and block access to hydrants.

As with any major catastrophe, the events, sights, sounds and emotions are permanently etched in memory for those who experienced them. For the Blizzard of 1978, perspective depends on location: for those near the coast, flooding dominated; inland, mountains of snow paralyzed entire communities.

For the majority of kids – even those in Rhode Island and Connecticut who were stranded overnight at school – the blizzard is a fond memory, mostly since classes were canceled for two weeks. The extended vacation resulted from both the treacherous driving conditions and the fact that many schools were being used as storm shelters and emergency command posts.

My father, Barry – a forward-thinking insurance man who had been recommending that coastal residents buy flood insurance for years – was among many community leaders who volunteered their time and talents for the disaster-relief effort. He quickly pressed my two brothers and me into service at the shelter set up at the elementary school not far from our house.

We got coffee for Red Cross workers, delivered paperwork between offices, and did whatever else needed to be done. Outside in the parking lot, we'd stare at the Army trucks, transports and helicopters in the way boys are awestruck by an up-close look at such heavy-duty military machinery. At home, we'd build snow forts and climb snow piles that seemed as high as Mount Everest.

It was a child's paradise, until the realization struck that there was a reason people were calling this event a "disaster." Once, after meeting a family still living in a school classroom, I asked why they didn't just go home. The impact of realizing that these people didn't have homes to go back to, and that those bundles of donated clothes and army blankets represented all their belongings, was profound, even for a seven-year-old.

Suddenly, the blizzard wasn't fun anymore.

The hiatus from reality was wearing thin, replaced by a desire for everyday life to return to normal. It would be weeks before that happened – the military helicopters whirring overhead and the soldiers patrolling the town's borders would be constant reminders of the disaster-recovery effort.

When school reopened, some classmates never returned; others came back for a short time but left when they moved from their temporary housing to more permanent living arrangements.

For many families, the effects of the Great Blizzard of 1978 lasted well beyond a few inconvenient days in February.

* * * * *

It's impossible to tell every story of every person who lived through the blizzard, but in these pages you'll experience the tragedy, the triumph, and even the humor from communities across New England.

Even with the passage of time, memories are vivid of the unexpected severity of the elements, the devastation of the coastline, the inability to move around, and acts of heroism and generosity during and after the storm.

Former Massachusetts Gov. Michael Dukakis, during an interview for this book, remembered leaving his State House office to buy a bowl of soup – "I was getting tired of eating bologna sandwiches" – and seeing a number of Bostonians gliding down Beacon Street on cross-country skis. "Everybody was out, getting to know their neighbors. Until then, many people didn't even know who these people were," he recounted. To this day, a woman to whom Dukakis gave "a half a buck to buy something at a convenience store" still thanks him for his generosity.

In the 25 years since the storm struck, Dukakis has been an active player on the local and national stage. Now a professor of political theory at Northeastern University, he served two more terms as governor (although sidelined for four years after a defeat in the fall of 1978), challenged George H. Bush for the presidency in 1988, and sits on the board of the Amtrak railroad system. Yet the Blizzard of 1978 ranks high among significant events in his career.

"Well, it's certainly a big one," he said. "It was a remarkable week."

So whether you spent the Storm of the Century with your family, among strangers at a shelter, shoveling mountains of snow, pumping water from your basement, or helping friends and neighbors get their lives back to normal, your story is important, too. Use this book as a springboard for sharing your experiences – even committing them to paper – so that future generations can better understand the enormity of what you, and thousands of New Englanders, endured 25 years ago.

Be proud of your memories. You survived the Blizzard of '78.

Christopher Haraden
February 2003

Chapter 1

The Elements Of A Disaster

"I don't think people in New England use information from winter storm forecasts to make these kind of preparations. We hear storm warnings every week, and sometimes they come and sometimes they don't."
— Rhode Island Gov. J. Joseph Garrahy,
in The Providence Journal, Feb. 12, 1978

The winter of 1978 occurred only 25 years ago, but it might well have been in another lifetime. Advances in meteorology, technology, and sociology in the new millennium have greatly improved our ability to predict, endure and survive natural disasters.

Imagine how different the impact of the storm would have been if cellular telephones were as commonplace as today, and residents had the advantage of up-to-the minute updates from the Internet or one of cable television's 24-hour news and weather channels? Or if the snowbound families who still had electricity could have passed the time by watching movies on their videocassette or digital video disc players?

In 1978, four-wheel-drive capability was generally reserved for pickups and large trucks – today, suburban driveways are filled with 4x4 sport-utility vehicles, some with all-wheel-drive sedans and station wagons.

Banks were closed for three days during the blizzard, and even those who could trek to their branch were out of luck – automated teller machines weren't yet widely available. "Storm orphans" stranded in shelters on their way home from work, or those who were plucked from the rooftops of their flooded homes, were left without access to their hard-earned money for days.

On the weather front, forecasters today have "a significant edge over 1978" because of more sophisticated computer models, new weather satellites and a nationwide network of Doppler radar systems, according to the National Weather Service. "The new technology, in addition to a highly skilled weather service work force, gives modern forecasting a significant edge over 1978," according to a statement the weather bureau issued in 1998 to mark the storm's 20th anniversary.

Despite these advances, New Englanders today are just as cavalier about the weather as they were a quarter-century ago. So the storm warnings of early February 1978 went mostly unheeded, even though a record-breaking snowstorm had buried the region only two weeks before.

With 21.4 inches of snow, the storm of Jan. 20-21 was, at the time, the largest total snowfall ever recorded in Boston. The mammoth accumulation was inconvenient, but not deadly, as it was not accompanied by high winds or astronomically high tides. Coastal flooding did occur, causing millions of dollars in damages, but most residents took the storm in stride.

For public officials charged with responding to emergency conditions, the heavy snow and flooding of January "provided a timely test of these and other state capabilities to respond effectively to emergency," Massachusetts Secretary of Public Safety Charles V. Barry wrote in a follow-up report on the 1978 winter season.

Few people anticipated how soon those capabilities would again be tested.

* * * * *

The Great Blizzard of 1978 developed as four distinct weather systems during the first weekend of February; by Monday evening the elements were in place for a storm that would shatter weather records.

On Friday, February 3, a weak low-pressure system was detected in the upper levels of the atmosphere in northern Canada, while another weak disturbance – a low-pressure area along the surface of the land – stretched from the Great Lakes to the Gulf of Mexico.

Each system brought snow along its route, with the ground-level low dropping flakes in Virginia and Pennsylvania, while the Canadian low picked up speed as it moved over the Great Lakes and into Ohio.

Another disturbance was detected on Sunday, February 5 as a "weak

Satellite images show the progression of the weather patterns that converged to become the Blizzard of 1978. Above, the storm is centered off the coast of southern New Jersey on Monday, Feb. 6, while all of New England is blanketed in clouds. Below, the storm is southeast of Cape Cod on Tuesday, Feb. 7. (Images provided by the U.S. Army Corps of Engineers.)

Satellite view of the United States on Feb. 7 shows the storm covering the Northeast, while in the view below, taken on Wednesday, Feb. 8, most of New England is under clear skies. (Images provided by the U.S. Army Corps of Engineers.)

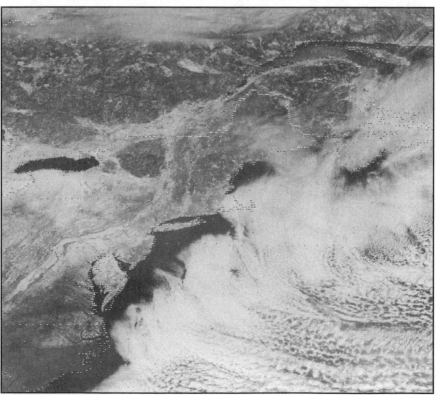

extratropical cyclone" off the South Carolina coast. Drawing on a plentiful supply of warm, moist air from the surface of the Atlantic Ocean, the low-pressure area gathered strength as it moved quickly westward.

It intensified further off the coast of Cape Hatteras, North Carolina, when it drained energy from the surface low that was weakening around Pennsylvania. As it began moving northeastward up the Eastern Seaboard, the National Weather Service issued warnings that labeled the storm an offshore gale, meaning the system had powerful sustained winds of between 34 and 47 miles per hour.

By 11:30 p.m. on Sunday night, the Weather Service's Boston bureau had issued a heavy snow watch and coastal gale warnings for Massachusetts, and predicted that rough surf and astronomically high tides would cause "considerable" beach erosion.

Forecasters all along the East Coast – from Virginia and Washington, D.C. to New Jersey and into upstate New York – were watching the same weather patterns and began warning of the potential for heavy snowfall and unusually high tides as early as Saturday. New York City, with a snow-removal budget already $12 million in the red from battling previous storms during the 1977-78 winter season, began preparing for the worst on Friday evening, after reviewing the forecast.

In Providence, the first winter storm watch was issued at 5 a.m. Sunday, with warnings of high winds in Narragansett Bay; 12 hours later, meteorologists upgraded the bulletin to a heavy snow watch (meaning six inches or more were expected) and issued gale warnings for all coastal areas.

Despite this activity in meteorological circles, the public was relatively unaware of the impending disaster – either because most forecasters were unsure of the exact intensity of the coming snow or because New Englanders traditionally shrug off predictions of severe weather until the storm is actually swirling around them.

Adding to the confusion, Rhode Islanders awoke Monday morning to discover only The Providence Journal on their front stoops, even though the paper's weather report predicted that snow should have begun dusting the city's doorsteps by 4 a.m. At daybreak, the skies were decidedly cloudy over the state's capital, and the first flakes wouldn't fall until close to 10 that morning. Many people, including Rhode Island's governor, thought the storm had changed course and moved into the Atlantic before reaching New England.

Just south of the Ocean State, moderate to heavy snow had begun in New Jersey and Delaware early Monday morning, and by sunrise, most

Commuters leaving work on Monday afternoon were confronted by blowing and drifting snow, which clogged streets and marooned some people for days. These images are from downtown Boston. (Frank Florianz photos)

of the Big Apple and Long Island were blanketed in white. Storm warnings from the Weather Service Office in Atlantic City were explicit: "In all honesty, if you needlessly travel at all today and are not prepared for the worst, you are putting your life on the line."

In Boston, the National Weather Service issued a "Special Weather

Statement for Massachusetts" at 6:30 a.m.: "Light snow will overspread our state this morning and continue this afternoon. While the snowfall today isn't expected to be very heavy, it will still be sufficient to cause some troubles for travelers, especially during the afternoon commuter hours.

"The snow will continue tonight and is expected to become heavy at times. In addition, strong and gusty northeasterly winds will cause considerable blowing and drifting of the snow. It is too early to say how much snow will fall but a substantial amount is indicated and travel will become difficult."

By noon, the NWS bulletins were more urgent: "Heavy snow or winter storm warnings are in effect this afternoon for most of the area from Maryland northeastward through central New England. The heaviest new snow ... generally accumulating between 8 and 16 inches ... is expected over most of the Middle Atlantic states, south coastal New York and Southern New England. Storm warnings are now posted along the Massachusetts and Rhode Island coasts, where there may be some coastal flooding and considerable beach erosion. Gale warnings are in effect elsewhere from Eastport, Maine to Virginia Beach, Virginia."

As these reports were being issued, the citizens of New England had already begun their daily routines. Commuters were at work, children had gone to school, and even politicians were tending to the mundane tasks of government.

Massachusetts Gov. Michael Dukakis sent state workers home early as a precaution, but still prepared for his scheduled appearance on a local radio show Monday evening. In Rhode Island, Gov. J. Joseph Garrahy and six other state officials left Providence early for Newport's Aquidneck Island, a trip that would leave them out of communication with the rest of state government for hours.

"The snow didn't materialize at that time," Garrahy said later. "Then that thought goes through your mind: 'How many times do they forecast snow and then the storm goes out to sea?'"

But the storm was not moving out to sea. In fact, when the Canadian low-pressure area collided with the coastal system just east of New Jersey on Monday evening, it fed even more energy into the storm.

A temperature difference of 110 degrees between the two air masses produced a vortex that drew warm water from the surface of the ocean up into cold air of the storm clouds, dumping snow at a rate of three inches an hour in some locations.

Typically, weather systems that follow this pattern travel at about 20

Some of the Massachusetts Bay Transportation Authority's Green Line trains run through city streets. The snow stopped many subway cars in their tracks, like this one on Commonwealth Avenue in Allston. (Frank Florianz photo)

miles per hour, meaning that New England would receive about eight or 10 inches of snow before the storm moved away from land.

The wild card, however, was the fourth weather element – an area of high pressure at the Canadian border that forced the huge bundle of energy to move at half its normal speed. Now hundreds of miles wide, the storm was labeled by one weather reporter as "a vast, vertical whirling dervish just off the New England coast" that appeared on satellites as "a cartwheel on the face of the sea."

This phenomenon is not uncommon, as at least two other significant snowstorms in New England's history resulted from "blocking" by Canadian high pressure – the Blizzard of 1888, which stalled over Block Island, and the 100-hour snowstorm of February 24-28, 1969, which was held in place off Cape Cod.

The key difference in 1978, however, was that the storm's duration included two full tide cycles and allowed high winds – blowing at near hurricane-force in many areas – to push waves from astronomically high tides farther and more forcefully onto the shore.

Not that the ocean needed any help. In an unfortunate meteorological coincidence, the winter storm occurred at the same time as other weather phenomena that produce higher-than-normal tides.

The moon, which controls the movement of oceans, was at its peri-

**Highest Snowfall Totals
Recorded in Boston**

27.1"   February 6-7, 1978
            Blizzard of 1978

26.3"   February 24-28, 1969
            "The 100 hour snowstorm."

25.4"   March 31-April 1, 1997
            Most snow in 24 hours, eclipsing the
            Blizzard of 1978's total of 23.6 inches.

21.4"   January 20-21, 1978

19.4"   February 16-17, 1958

18.7"   February 8-10, 1994

18.2"   January 7-8, 1996

gee – or the closest point in its orbit of the earth – on Sunday, Feb. 5. The closeness of the moon results in a stronger influence on tides, with the maximum effect about two and a half days after the perigee occurs. At the same time, a new moon on Tuesday would produce "spring tides," which also are higher than average.

If the perigean spring tides weren't enough, the blizzard arrived in the middle of a "nodal tide" cycle in early February. Nodal tides, which are higher and have faster currents, occur once every 18.6 years, when the orbital planes of the moon and the earth are in a particular alignment.

With the meteorological elements setting the stage for intense flooding, coastal residents braced for the worst. And the worst was soon upon them.

The low tide on Monday afternoon crested 2.6 feet higher than was anticipated, prompting warnings that the coming high tide, which occurred at 10:20 p.m. in Boston Harbor, would surely be disastrous.

"Strong easterly winds will push tides two to four feet above normal and, when coupled with already high astronomical tides, will cause extensive flooding of low-lying coastal areas for several hours around the time of high tide tonight and Tuesday morning," the National Weather Service warned in an 8 p.m. bulletin.

Emergency workers, like this fire department crew in Rhode Island, were hampered by the snow, which fell at the rate of three inches per hour at the height of the storm. (Providence Journal photo)

The rising tide pushed through the snow cover in coastal areas like Rockport Harbor, above, sending ice floes floating along the water's surface. (U.S. Army Corps of Engineers photo)

"Any preparation for such flooding should be rushed to completion within the next hour or so … the sustained strong east and northeast winds will cause the sea to pile up along our coastal areas, resulting in widespread beach erosion and pounding of sea walls. Coastal roads will be frequently washed by the breaking surf and some during high tide Tuesday morning will be under water."

Many residents were evacuated to storm shelters, fighting strong east and northeasterly winds that had blown snow into drifts several feet high in some areas. The storm's highest sustained winds were reported at 51 miles per hour, while the wind gusted to greater-than-hurricane-strength at Chatham (92 miles per hour) and Logan International Airport in Boston (75 mph, just higher than hurricane-force of 74 mph). On Mount Washington in New Hampshire, gusts reached 125 mph, while gusts approached 100 mph at Newburyport's Plum Island.

High tide Monday night saw an incredible surge of 10.1 feet above normal, tying the record in Boston set on April 14, 1851. At 7 p.m., water began washing over the sea walls in the Beachmont section of Revere; the wind-driven waves poured over walls and sand dunes in other coastal communities like Winthrop, Marshfield, Scituate, Sandwich and Provincetown. Power lines toppled and basements flooded.

Commuters rushing to get home crowded city buses like this one at Dorrance Street in Providence. Some buses never made it to their destinations, forcing riders to seek shelter in buildings around the city. (Providence Journal photo)

Cars, furniture and anything that wasn't nailed down floated through the streets. People clung to their porches – and some retreated to the roof – to wait for help to arrive.

At 10 p.m., the storm was just south of the eastern tip of Long Island, and by midnight, 8.1 inches of snow had fallen. The flood waters diminished somewhat as the tides receded, but in places like Hull, the sea walls and sand dunes had the opposite of their intended effect, preventing the water from returning to the ocean.

By dawn Tuesday, little had changed: "During the night, the storm moved only slowly eastward … centered at 5 a.m. in the vicinity of Cape Cod. Not much improvement is expected in the weather conditions across the state until the storm moves well away from New England later today," the weather service reported.

"Simply, stay at home," an 8:45 a.m. NWS bulletin read. "For several hours prior to and following high tide this morning, extensive flooding of coastal areas is likely. Those who may have returned to shore front property following last night's evacuation are urged to seek the safety of high ground before the rising tide once again inundates coastal areas."

The morning tide of 10.4 feet was even worse than expected, smashing the previous record and smashing into the shore with unrelenting fury. Coastal residents who hadn't abandoned their homes kept rescuers busy throughout the day, and the number of refugees in shelters swelled into the thousands.

The National Weather Service's dispatches began to sound more hopeful beginning at 11:45 a.m. Tuesday, when the weather update carried the headline, "Skies brighten on a stricken state."

"Although most sections of Massachusetts are still in the iron grips of the worst winter storm in recent history, skies are brightening as the snow shows signs of gradually tapering off," the weather service said.

"Coastal flooding … will diminish early this afternoon as tides back off from record or near-record highs. Another period of flooding may be expected during the period of high tide tonight … but winds should be lighter and from a more northwesterly direction so that the flooding should not be as extreme or as severe…"

The storm center, which had stalled near Nantucket, began moving eastward late Tuesday morning and picked up speed during the afternoon. Wind speeds decreased, and later high tides, although still above normal, were more manageable.

Snow began tapering off at noon, and finally ended at 10 p.m. The

The streets of downtown Providence resembled a demolition derby on Monday afternoon as motorists scrambled to get out of the city. Many were forced to abandon their cars and seek shelter. (Providence Journal photo)

The snow was still blowing hard Tuesday, piling up around the cars and trucks that were stopped in their tracks on Route 195 eastbound, along the Washington Bridge in Providence. (Providence Journal photo)

storm's total accumulation of 27.1 inches in Boston (measured at Logan Airport) is a record that still stands. At the time, the Blizzard of 1978 also held the record for the most snowfall in 24 hours – 23.6 inches – but a snowstorm on March 31-April 1, 1997 surpassed that record by 1.8 inches.

By the time the snow ended on Tuesday, the New York metropolitan area had received 14 to 20 inches of snow, while northern New Jersey was digging out from under two feet. Midtown Manhattan reported 17.7 inches, the sixth greatest accumulation since recordkeeping began in 1869.

The still-active storm then moved into the North Atlantic, where ships reported winds of 75 miles per hour and 20-foot waves. By Thursday, the weather system had traveled east of Newfoundland, and mariners reported swells of 30 feet. The storm would remain intense, zigzagging through the North Atlantic shipping lanes and finally dissipating on Feb. 13, a full week after it had begun pummeling the eastern United States.

* * * * *

Weather watchers may debate the merits of other storms that have buffeted the area, but none had the paralyzing effect of the bundle of weather that slammed into the region like an out-of-control freight train in February 1978. Record-breaking snowfall, near-hurricane force winds with gusts of more than 100 miles per hour, 10-foot tides that splintered houses and reduced concrete sea walls to rubble – never before, and never since, have all of these forces of nature combined to devastate New England.

But what makes the blizzard truly the storm of the century is its aftermath. The entire states of Massachusetts, Rhode Island and Connecticut were shut down for days. Soldiers patrolled streets and enforced curfews. Thousands of cars were abandoned on highways, and thousands more people spent days in shelters. Landmarks that had withstood the tests of other storms toppled. Even Ash Wednesday was postponed. Neighbors pulled together to help each other in a show of extraordinary community spirit. Everyone who lived through the blizzard remembers exactly where he or she was when the storm hit.

It snows every winter in New England, but only one storm qualifies as the Storm of the Century for the 1900s – the Great Blizzard of 1978.

Chapter 2

A Long Day's Journey Into Night

"It was a mean and violent week because the Blizzard of '78 was a two-headed demon.

"First came the snow. Even at the start there was an unusual bite to it, a sting. It began early Monday morning and a few hours later was striking the ground with an audible hiss.

"By noon it had killed a man and by mid-afternoon people were in flight. By late afternoon a mighty whistling wind had pushed it into great drifts that made everything stop.

"And then, after night had come and no one could see it, the sea went mad in a way it has seldom gone mad before, chewing and spitting what man had built at its edge.

"In the morning the bits and pieces lay on the beach like all the wreckage of the world. What the sea did was the worst of all."

— Boston Herald American, Sunday, Feb. 12, 1978

D espite the long advance notice, thousands of people ... didn't move soon enough last Monday, and soon enough they weren't moving at all," was how The Providence Journal described the snarled commute that turned highways into snow-covered parking lots all over New England on Feb. 6.

In Providence, the intensity of the snow and the sheer number of cars on the road – nearly all of the city's businesses released their employees between 1 p.m. and 2 p.m. – prevented public-works crews from clearing the streets. Along Routes 95 and 195, it was not uncommon to see a plow truck buried in the snow among hundreds of cars.

Nobody was immune from the traffic jams that snarled the region's highways. The truck in the top center of this photo of Route 128 in Needham has a plow attached! (U.S. Army Corps of Engineers photo)

In Massachusetts, major backups were caused by tractor-trailers that jackknifed on slippery roads. On Monday afternoon, an 18-wheeler blocked Route 9 in Southborough, stranding approximately 1,400 cars. Motorists snacked on cases of Hostess Twinkies unloaded from a delivery truck on the highway until snowmobilers and other rescue crews

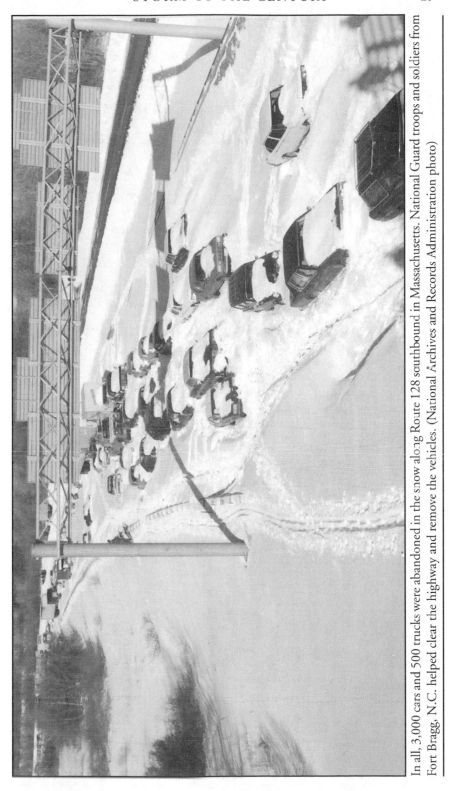

In all, 3,000 cars and 500 trucks were abandoned in the snow along Route 128 southbound in Massachusetts. National Guard troops and soldiers from Fort Bragg, N.C. helped clear the highway and remove the vehicles. (National Archives and Records Administration photo)

Boston Herald American photographer Kevin Cole captured this view of Route 128 during a helicopter trip across the South Shore. The newspaper's photography staff won the Pulitzer Prize that year for outstanding coverage of the blizzard. (Kevin Cole/ Boston Herald photo)

Jackknifed tractor trailers stopped traffic along Route 128 at rush hour Monday afternoon, and soon the heavy snow had drifted around the stalled cars. (U.S. Army Corps of Engineers photo)

brought the stranded to area shelters.

Several hundred cars became trapped on Route 16 in Milford, and there were between 300 and 500 vehicles on the Massachusetts Turnpike between Southborough and Framingham. Drivers marooned on the Pike were shuttled to shelters by a group of about 20 hardy souls known as the Southborough Snowburrows, who ran rescue missions on their snowmobiles.

Probably the most famous traffic tie-up was along an eight-mile stretch of Route 128, southbound between Needham and Canton. During rush hour, "two tractor-trailers attempting to negotiate a grade jackknifed into positions completely blocking the artery," state Department of Public Works Commissioner John J. Carroll wrote in a follow-up report on the blizzard. Carroll noted that many other Massachusetts highways became paralyzed as weather-related accidents blocked lanes. Wind-blown snow drifted around the stalled cars, and many drivers simply gave up, abandoning their autos altogether or settling in until rescuers arrived. In all, 3,000 cars and 500 trucks were stranded on Route 128 Monday night.

Unsure of what to do, drivers and their passengers slept in shifts,

Footprints through the snow show where State Troopers, tow-truck drivers and other good Samaritans spent the night walking the highways, checking on motorists trapped in their cars. (U.S. Army Corps of Engineers photo)

turning car engines on and off to conserve gas and occasionally venturing outside to clear snow from the tailpipe. State troopers, tow-truck drivers and other good Samaritans spent the night walking the highways, checking on the occupants of cars and delivering messages that help was on the way.

On the radio, Massachusetts Gov. Michael Dukakis fielded questions from constituents during his monthly "town meeting" show with WHDH's David Brudnoy. Between questions about taxation, budget cuts and the economy, Dukakis took off-air calls from key staff members, who warned him that the state was under siege by the weather.

"People were calling in with the regular monthly stuff, and then the storm started getting worse," Dukakis said. "I think it was Charlie [Barry, secretary of public safety] who called me at the studio and said, 'This is going to be a lot more serious that we thought it was.' So I said, 'Tell me what you need me to say,' and that's when I began to try to communicate with folks, in this case, over this one radio station."

First, the governor asked residents along the coast, especially low-lying areas like Winthrop, to evacuate their homes before the next high tide, which was about an hour away. At 9:38 p.m., Dukakis took Barry's advice and used the radio broadcast to declare a state of emergency.

With nowhere else to go, people who lived near the highways gathered on overpasses to watch as Army personnel began clearing the roads. On Route 128, troops first plowed the northbound lane, then removed the guard rail at one-mile intervals and pulled cars across the highway. The process took several days to complete. (U.S. Army Corps of Engineers photos)

A huge double-bladed plow cuts through snow drifts on Belcher Avenue in Brockton on Feb. 9. (Stanley Bauman photo)

Within a half-hour, he ordered the entire Massachusetts National Guard to storm duty.

Along Route 128, some drivers sought shelter at schools, churches, armories, office buildings and even private homes. In Dedham, neighbors on Vincent Rd. opened their homes to about 300 refugees from the highway; some residents brought hot drinks to those who elected to stay with their cars.

The Red Cross established a disaster center at the Showcase Cinemas on Route 1, accommodating at least 500 people for nearly three days. The trapped crowd saw continuous showings of the movies "Julia" and "Gauntlet" during their stay. In Needham, St. Bartholemew's Church housed 1,200 people in church and school buildings; at least 100 people took shelter in several locations in Norwood.

The state's Civil Defense Agency launched a rescue effort, ordering Department of Public Works snowplows and Massachusetts Bay Transportation Authority buses to travel parts of Route 128 and bring people to shelters. Drivers flashed their headlights as the trucks approached, hoping to be seen through the blinding snow. Others decided to take their chances, believing that the traffic jam would clear itself up in a few hours. At least four people died from carbon monoxide poisoning while stranded in their cars in various parts of the state.

By the time the snow had stopped Tuesday night, cars all over Boston were buried under more than two feet of snow. These vehicles are waiting to be shoveled out in Allston. (Frank Florianz photo)

The governor banned most cars from the roads for days after the storm, so some Bostonians used their cross-country skis to travel the snow-packed streets. Above, skiiers glide along the Green Line trolley tracks in the middle of Commonwealth Ave. (Frank Florianz photos)

In Providence, the city's only two major hotels, the Holiday Inn and the Marriott, were filled with refugees from the highways or passengers from city buses that became stuck in traffic. Hotel staff members handed out sheets and blankets so that "guests" sleeping in the lobby and in the hallways would be warm.

The volume of snow made it difficult to effectively plow residential neighborhoods in Boston, as the above view in Allston demonstrates, but streets without cars, such as near the Prudential Center, below, cleaned up more easily, (Frank Florianz photos)

As the snow continued falling into the night, churches, factories, hospitals and office buildings all over the city became makeshift shel-

ters. More than 600 people took refuge at the Civic Center, and 400 more were at the Spiedel manufacturing plant on Ship St.

"We have made a survey of the entire state and everything is negative," Civil Defense Director Santo Amato told The Providence Journal. "No city or town has passable highways. We have shelters loaded with people and every public building that is open is serving as a shelter."

Commuters from shoreline towns in the Bay State had no better luck than their counterparts on land, as The Boston Herald American reported that riders aboard Monday night's Boston-to-Hingham ferry "spent 40 hours together, but there were no problems. The bar was well stocked and there was enough canned spaghetti and frozen fried chicken to go around."

The boat that shuttled passengers between Rowes Wharf in Boston and Pemberton Pier in Hull pulled into port about an hour later than scheduled on Monday evening. Capt. Norman Rogers, a retired

Car owners in the city found it necessary to mark their territory, as vehicles buried under snow became invisible to plow drivers. This 'car here' sign was posted on Bellvista Road in Allston. (Frank Florianz photo)

Coast Guard commander, piloted the Nantascot through the choppy waters and high winds, following the shoreline more closely than usual.

The 80 passengers aboard braved rough seas and were grateful to have made it back onto dry land, but faced the perilous task of getting home from Pemberton Pier, located at the northernmost tip of the Hull peninsula. It was still several hours from high tide, but the ocean began pouring over seawalls and down side streets in the early evening, isolating many parts of town.

For these commuters and other coastal residents, a long night of challenges was just beginning.

* * * * *

"During the storm's early stages the majority of Massachusetts communities felt capable of coping with the results of the blizzard," Barry,

Walking along city streets presented a whole new set of obstacles after the blizzard. (Frank Florianz photo)

Digging out from the record-breaking snowfall in Boston created a new set of problems – how to park cars among the massive snow piles. (Frank Florianz photo)

Days after the snow stopped, plows had yet to reach every street in every neighborhood. Above, Allston residents begin the long process of clearing the street. (Frank Florianz photo)

Mayor Kevin White's 'Little City Halls' in Boston neighborhoods -- the Allston-Brighton facility is shown above -- provided help to residents seeking disaster-relief information. (Frank Florianz photo)

Frustrated residents of Cranston, R.I. etched out a message in the snow with their footprints. (Providence Journal photo)

The residents of Morse Avenue in Brockton might have sent the same message, as their street had yet to be plowed by Wednesday afternoon. (Stanley Bauman photo)

the secretary of public safety, remarked in a report to Dukakis. "Indeed, it was not until Monday evening that municipal governments began to perceive the magnitude of the storm. At this point, requests for assistance began to arrive at various state agencies."

Revere, Winthrop, Hull, Quincy and Marshfield - all waterfront communities – were the first to ask for help evacuating residents. MBTA buses were sent to Point Shirley in Winthrop, but had to turn back because of the rising tide. Two amphibious vehicles (called "ducks") were sent instead. Another duck, nicknamed "Donald," was dispatched to the Beachmont section of Revere, while Army personnel carriers from Fort Devens were sent to Hull.

Monday night's high tide was an incredible 10.1 feet above normal, sending ocean water into areas that had never before flooded. According to a National Weather Service bulletin at 10:45 p.m., five feet of water blocked the Southeast Expressway where it crosses the Neponset River in Milton. Some sections of Revere were reportedly inundated with as much as 20 feet of water.

"Twice each day, I thought I was going to die," Revere resident Anthony Chiarella told The Boston Globe. Chiarella spent nearly two days in his attic with his dog, Sergeant, before rescuers reached him Wednesday afternoon. "The water came down the street like I've never seen it come before. It didn't just leak into the house, it came blasting in. It broke up my furniture and ripped up my house."

Rescues in coastal neighborhoods would continue through the night, as the flood waters never seemed to recede. For these storm victims, the state's Civil Defense Agency opened shelters in schools and National Guard armories around the state.

Residents with Citizens Band (CB) radios were active throughout the storm and the aftermath, helping relief workers identify trouble spots and relaying messages to stranded residents. Lillian Willis and Joanne Fallon, who managed the cafeteria at Hull's storm shelter at the Memorial Middle School, credited CBers with obtaining food and other supplies for the kitchen. Elsewhere in New England, the CB radio community was praised for being a "lifeline" during the disaster.

In the Pemberton section of Hull, members of the Murphy family were spending their first winter in their cottage on Channel St. When the waves battered the house and tore away the front stairs, they braved waist-deep water to reach a neighbor's home.

From there, they watched fire destroy two houses on Town Way. Firefighters reached the burning building, but discovered that the hy-

As soon as the snow stopped, front-end loaders began clearing mountains of snow from the exit ramps of highways in and around New England's major cities. The absence of cars kept the snow cover pristine on most roads, like Route 2 in Boston, below. (Frank Florianz photos)

drants were under water. Riding an Army transport, firefighters plucked the residents from the porch of the house, and brought them to the nearby Point Allerton Coast Guard Station.

The ocean damaged cottages, sea walls and roads in New Hampshire's Seacoast region, forcing the evacuation of about 150 year-round resi-

Most of the town of Hull was under water when high tides spilled over sand dunes and sea walls to flood homes and float cars out of their driveways. It took more than a week to pump the remaining water from the town's low-lying streets, like Wilson Ave. (now Hadassah Way), above, and Brewster St., below. (Rosalyn Glikin Simons photos)

Minot's Ledge Lighthouse, off the coast of Scituate, was pounded by the ocean waves during the blizzard. The lighthouse is known as 'lovers' light' because its beacon flashes in a 1-4-3 sequence. (Kevin Cole/Boston Herald photo)

Cars clogging Rhode Island's highways, like Route 95 above, formed a maze in the snow, making cleanup efforts difficult. (Providence Journal photo)

Public works crews eventually cleared the roads leading into and out of Boston, but with a ban on travel in effect for a week, there was no one to use them. (Frank Florianz photos)

The Providence Journal noted that the snow-covered cars blocking the interchange of Routes 95 and 195 'shows why transportation in metropolitan Providence is at a standstill.' (Providence Journal photo)

Route 95 northbound in Pawtucket is covered with snow on the Tuesday of the storm. (Providence Journal photo)

The blizzard interrupted everyone's routines, from man's best friend (above) to the Massachusetts Bay Transportation Authority Police, whose cruiser became bogged down on a Boston street. (Frank Florianz photos)

dents in Hampton. The state's National Guard provided cots and blankets for the shelter's overnight guests, which included 13 dogs and seven cats.

Power outages were reported throughout the region, with nearly 100,000 Boston Edison customers losing electricity during the storm. Much of the coast was also without power, as the surging seas toppled utility poles and snapped wires. Approximately 900 people in Scituate,

Mass. were without lights for a week, while another 2,500 houses and businesses in Duxbury, Plymouth, Marshfield and Bourne were in the dark for several days before crews could replace the damaged poles. On Cape Cod, about 4,000 customers, mostly in Orleans and Provincetown, briefly lost power on Monday night.

Rhode Island's Narragansett Electric Co. reported that high winds knocked out power to 10,000 customers, 4,000 of them in Warwick. While linemen hitched rides on snowplows to reach the trouble spots, by Wednesday morning the electric company had issued a request for help from snowmobile owners to bring work crews to remote areas.

* * * * *

Tragedy struck early during the blizzard, as the first of 54 deaths attributed to the storm occurred Monday afternoon. Ronald G. Thompson, a Massachusetts Department of Public Works employee, was killed when a car skidded into his truck on Route 128. Other deaths resulted from heart attacks, carbon monoxide poisoning, or drowning.

In Scituate, five year-old Amy Lanzikos and 62-year-old Edward Hart drowned when a rescue boat capsized on Jericho Rd. The girl's mother and Hart's wife, also in the boat, were rescued by firefighters. In Hanson, 15-year-old Donna Lee Porter was electrocuted when she stepped on a power line that was buried under the snow.

On the Bay State's North Shore, five men aboard the "Can Do" pilot boat were lost at sea Monday night. Capt. Frank Quirk had set out from Gloucester to reach the Global Hope, a 682-foot tanker that ran aground about a half-mile offshore in Salem Harbor. The Coast Guard initially couldn't reach the 32 crewmen on the Greek ship, which was carrying 160,000 gallons of oil, so Quirk and his crew - Donald Wilkinson, David Curley, Kenneth Fuller and

This parking meter in downtown Boston is in 'violation' mode, but can anyone get there to issue a ticket? (Frank Florianz photo)

To fight 'cabin fever,' many residents took to the streets of Boston, even if they didn't have a firm destination. (Frank Florianz photos)

Charles Bucko - made a rescue attempt at about 7:30 p.m. Monday.

Contact with the Can Do was lost at about 3 a.m. Tuesday, and the bodies of the five men washed ashore the next day. On Wednesday, the Coast Guard evacuated 28 of the Global Hope's crew; the last four men stayed with the ship, which was leaking oil into Salem Sound.

States of emergency were declared in Massachusetts, Rhode Island and Connecticut and New Hampshire, but Connecticut Gov. Ella

Can you guess where the state line is? The Massachusetts side of Route 195 was plowed to the Rhode Island border, but no further. (Providence Journal photo)

Forest Street in Brockton appeared to be a pedestrian thoroughfare as residents traveled to the West Side Shopping Center on foot. (Stanley Bauman photo)

Grasso was the first to take the drastic step of shutting down her state.

"Effective at 10 p.m. tonight, Monday, February 6th, I am ordering that all roads and highways in our state be closed to all motor vehicles except the following: Vehicles engaged in clearing roads, emergency vehicles assisting state agencies in emergencies and private vehicles on emergency missions," the governor declared. "I am asking all businesses, industries, schools, service firms, and all persons and companies not engaged in emergency activities to voluntarily suspend operations."

Grasso also had asked owners of four-wheel-drive vehicles to contact their local Civil Defense office or nearest State Police troop; on Tuesday morning, she asked 4x4 vehicle owners to call hospitals and nursing homes and offer transportation for nurses and doctors.

* * * * *

The light of day Tuesday morning brought no relief from the snow, the wind, or the water. By the mid-morning high tide in Boston, snow was still falling at the rate of a half-inch per hour, and winds were blowing hard at 31 mph.

"Storm orphans" who spent the night at shelters along the region's highways awoke to the realization that they would be stranded for some time. Families who left their homes to escape the rising tide were fortunate to miss the all-time high in Boston: 10.4 feet above normal.

Officials kept cars off the road as long as possible so that cleanup crews could do their work. Even as the driving restrictions were lifted, residents were encouraged to use public buses and trolleys as alternative transportation. (Frank Florianz photos)

One newspaper in Maine called the ferocious surf the "monster on the beaches."

"Walter A. George's ranch-type home on Two Lights Road in Cape Elizabeth has a wonderful view of the ocean, but no one would have traded places with him last Tuesday," The Maine Sunday Telegraph reported on Feb. 12. "As surging, pounding surf racked the one-story structure, George and a neighbor worked desperately to save as many furnishings as possible. Suddenly, they spotted a huge wave rolling to-

Snow drifts several feet high left Michael Barron with few options except to climb atop a snowbound telephone in downtown Brockton. (Stanley Bauman photo)

Letita Round is helped through the snow by Brockton patrolman John F. Reardon. (Stanley Bauman photo)

---

ward the house. George had just time to grab his cat and duck before the Atlantic Ocean came pouring into his living room."

In Kennebunk Beach, Maine, 25-foot waves crashed into homes along the shoreline.

"I was clearing ice from the drains under my sea wall, so the breaking seas could drain out instead of eating away the underpinnings," David Hall of Lord's Point told the Sunday Telegraph. "I glanced over my shoulder, and suddenly saw that monster wave coming at me, I think 25 to 35 feet high, hundreds of feet wide ... It swept me away like a hunk of seaweed: swirled me among all the flotsam and ice in its grip. I was dumped high on a snow bank. I'd been swept off to the side, then behind my house and across the street."

The highways, airports and public transit systems across New England were at standstill, buried under nearly three feet of snow. Dukakis followed Grasso's lead and banned all private driving in Massachusetts at 10 a.m. Tuesday. In Providence, Mayor Vincent Cianci went a step further, banning both pedestrians and autos from the city.

"We are going to arrest people who insist on joy-riding," Cianci warned in an interview with The Providence Journal. "Their cars will be towed away on the spot. Of course, if you're taking your mother who has a heart attack to the hospital, then that's another thing."

Connecticut's Gold Star Memorial Bridges, which carry the north-

With no place else to put the snow cleared from highways and city streets, Rhode Island's DPW crews dumped the snow into the Providence River. (Providence Journal photo)

and southbound lanes of Route 95 over the Thames River between New London and Groton, were eerily empty Tuesday morning, as was Eugene O'Neill Blvd. in downtown New London. Only a few abandoned cars dotted the roads, which were buried under snowdrifts several feet high.

The chief executives of New Hampshire, Massachusetts, Rhode Island and Connecticut all sought disaster declarations from President Jimmy Carter to give them direct access to military assistance. As a result, soldiers and equipment from Fort Bragg, North Carolina, as well as personnel from the Army Corps of Engineers, joined the snow removal and coastal rescue effort in Massachusetts. Soldiers from Fort Benning, Georgia were deployed to Rhode Island.

State and local officials quickly prioritized their emergency responses, putting food deliveries and medical issues first on the list. Patients needing kidney dialysis, chemotherapy treatment or other medical attention were transported by the military; doctors, nurses and medical technicians were escorted to work or brought out in the field to administer aid.

The National Guard delivered water pumps and more than 100,000 sandbags to coastal areas where sea walls had collapsed; Army personnel assisted state highway workers in clearing snow and stalled cars.

Beginning Wednesday morning, tow trucks and bulldozers worked methodically to remove vehicles from Route 128 near the Highland Ave. exit. After the northbound lane was plowed, workers removed sections of the guardrail at one-mile intervals and brought the stranded cars across from the southbound side.

Providence officials purposely blocked onramps with mounds of snow and police patrols to stop people from entering the city while the cleanup was under way.

Relief agencies weren't the only ones cooperating to help storm victims. Stores and restaurants stayed open late, some all night long, to feed plow drivers and provide food for area residents. WKOX in Framingham and WGTR in Natick, normally daytime radio stations, stayed on the air around the clock to keep storm-isolated residents in touch with each other and to help find volunteers to help with snow shoveling and emergency services. Neighbors helped each other more than ever and forged lasting bonds during the crisis.

This spirit of community was the legacy of the blizzard's aftermath.

Boston Globe sportswriter Leigh Montville, in a post-storm article in Yankee magazine, noted increased goodwill among his suburban

Brown University student Elaine Zeman took the driving ban seriously, using Interstate 95 as a pedestrian passageway to Rhode Island Hospital, where she worked. Although now a professor of Radiation Oncology at the University of North Carolina School of Medicine, she reports still rushing out to buy milk, juice and bread once she hears the word 'snow' in a weather forecast. (Photo courtesy of Elaine Zeman)

neighbors, although he acknowledged that the camaraderie likely would not survive the spring thaw:

"I met neighbors I had never seen before. It was as if we now had something we could say to each other. There was a meaningful subject for discussion. People came past on cross-country skis. People dragged sleds everywhere. People rang the doorbell to say they were going to the store and wanted to know if they could buy anything for us. A week earlier they wouldn't have said hello on the street, driving past in their cars. I drank beer on a Wednesday afternoon with a couple from the next street over. There was no rush, no obligation. None of us had to work.

" 'We should do this more often,' I said.

" 'We *should* do this more often,' the neighbors agreed.

"We all knew this would never happen."

Once highways became clear, motorists joined the effort to move the thousands of stranded cars. This vehicle was along Route 195 eastbound in Providence. (Providence Journal photo)

Police officers checked the identifications of all vehicles entering cities with driving bans. A tow-truck driver checks in with a police guard in Providence. (Providence Journal photo)

The message on the snow monkey poster hanging at the Providence YMCA seemed to sum up the feelings of those stranded in makeshift shelters across the region. Below, refugees at the Holiday Inn in Providence look for some storm news on television. (Providence Journal photos)

Shoppers who ventured out to the markets got mixed results, depending on whether delivery trucks were able to reach the stores. Above, the shelves were cleared at the Star Market at University Heights in Providence on Thursday, while the Brockton Public Market was restocked with bread and other staples on Friday. (Top: Providence Journal photo; bottom: Stanley Bauman photo)

James Brower of Brockton wheels shopping carts back to the Brockton Public Market through the store's parking lot, which is surrounded by mountains of snow. (Stanley Bauman photo)

National Guard troops helped area residents obtain food, either by making deliveries themselves or delivering the people directly to the markets. (Stanley Bauman photo)

Chapter 3

Dukakis: The Calm Amid The Storm

To many, he was an unlikely hero: the cerebral, policy-wonk governor whom critics labeled cold and aloof, already under fire for slashing budgets and raising taxes in his first years in Massachusetts' corner office.

But when disaster struck in early February 1978, a series of television appearances radically transformed the button-down image of Gov. Michael S. Dukakis.

Dressed casually, with a black turtleneck shirt under his sweater, Dukakis first hit the airwaves of the major TV stations on Tuesday morning. For days, the unflappable governor gave a much-needed personal touch to important storm bulletins and was a lifeline of information for local officials and residents.

Most significantly, his calming presence assured an anxious public that everything was going to be all right.

In retrospect, Dukakis isn't philosophical about his famous "sweater speeches," which biographers have called "the kind of sustained positive publicity that politicians dream about."

"Well, I'm not sure you sit around thinking broad philosophical thoughts," Dukakis said in a recent interview. "You've got a job to do; you've got a state that's in trouble, and people don't know what to do, so they're looking at you. People would say, 'I've got to tune in and see what the governor is going to say now.' It's a pretty awesome responsibility.

"TV was the medium. It was enormously important and enormously helpful," Dukakis said. Then, recalling that he had banned all nonessential driving, he added, "Of course, there were newspapers, but how could you get a newspaper?"

To this day, blizzard survivors remember that once power was restored, the first thing they saw on television was Dukakis, who appeared calm, compassionate, and firmly in charge.

He pleaded with residents to conserve fuel, offered details about the progress of snow-removal efforts, and demonstrated a genuine concern for the well-being of citizens.

Former Massachusetts Gov. Michael Dukakis.

"I know that some of you are suffering from cabin fever or are getting a little stir crazy sitting around the house," he said during a live press conference broadcast Thursday afternoon, Feb. 9. "I hope you will just remember that we have some people in this state that barely escaped with their lives, that are sitting homeless and in very, very desperate straits."

While the governor was the public face of the emergency response team, Dukakis said former Secretary of Public Safety Charles V. Barry

The Massachusetts State House on Beacon Hill was blanketed in snow during the blizzard. Dukakis shuttled between his corner office and a command post at the Metropolitan District Commission headquarters nearby. (Frank Florianz photo)

To promote Hull Appreciation Day, an event held during the summer of 1978 to thank disaster-relief workers in Hull, Dukakis posed with, from left, state Rep. Caroline Stouffer, state Sen. Allan McKinnon, and Appreciation Day co-Chairman Barry Haraden (the author's father). Read more about Appreciation Day and the bumper stickers they're holding on pages 119-120. (Photo courtesy of Barry Haraden)

deserves the real credit for developing the state's disaster plan. Barry, who Dukakis described as "absolutely obsessed with emergency planning, when most of us [in state government] kind of passed it off," had briefed top cabinet officials on disaster response issues in early January of 1978.

When the storm struck a month later, state officials were prepared, and implemented Barry's comprehensive plan. Dukakis relied heavily on the advice of Barry, who had been a 37-year veteran of the Boston Police Department and served as the top public-safety officer during each of Dukakis' three terms as governor.

"I didn't go out there and say the first thing that came into my head," Dukakis said. "It was always, 'Charlie, what can we say now? What can we tell people? How much can they do, and how much can't they do? Where are the danger areas?'

"You're concerned about making sure that the information you are giving is accurate, and that you don't make some dumb mistake, which is another reason why you have to rely very heavily on the people you depend on to be the experts."

In times of crisis, citizens expect their political leaders to take charge, said Dukakis, whom The Boston Globe called "the state's news anchor-

A winding path through Boston Common was one of the few ways to get around the city in the early days after the blizzard. (Frank Florianz photo)

man of the week."

"Typically, it's someone in elected office, at some level," said Dukakis. "It's just a reminder that this isn't some theoretical thing, or something you pick up in a public management textbook. It's absolutely critical."

Although widely praised for his performance during the blizzard, Dukakis was defeated in the Democratic primary only nine months later. He reclaimed the governor's office after unseating his nemesis, Edward King, in 1982, and completed another eight years, becoming the longest-serving chief executive in Massachusetts history.

Political observers have long debated the reasons for the 1978 election results, but Dukakis offered a tongue-in-cheek explanation from former state Senate President William Bulger, who blamed the governor's decision to shut down most of the state during the blizzard.

"He said that keeping husbands and wives in the same house for a week was what did me in, because after a while, they started taking it out on me."

* * * * *

Dukakis' televised speeches were remembered for the way in which they blended the delivery of vital information and the acknowledgment that surviving the blizzard was not easy for residents. Below is the text of his speech on Thursday, Feb. 9:

    It appears over the course of the past 24 hours that we have a very long way to go. Most of our secondary roads still are impassable. I've talked with some mayors who tell me that their communities may take as much as a week or more to get back to anything reasonably near normal.

So the state of emergency will continue in effect through at least midnight on Friday – with some significant changes.

To begin with, in addition to the exemption that we granted last night to communities in western Massachusetts, all of Barnstable County will now be exempt from the state of emergency. Approximately 40 communities in central Massachusetts, including Worcester and Framingham, will be exempt and any other community whose mayor or board of selectmen would like to be exempted from the state of emergency should get in touch with Bob Cunningham, our Civil Defense director, to discuss it with him.

On the other hand, we cannot guarantee the lifting of such an exemption for obvious reasons because in many cases we have communities which may believe internally that they are capable of functioning now with a reasonably close to normal level, but in fact they are in a region that is in serious trouble and we simply cannot have people out in their cars and moving around and crossing the community lines as inevitably they will.

So that with the exception of those central Massachusetts communities, Barnstable County and other communities which are exempted by specific order of the Civil Defense director, the state of emergency will continue in effect.

Now, supermarkets and drugstores will remain open and they will be exempted from the Blue Laws on Sunday, so that supermarkets will be open on Sunday. People will be able to purchase food and supplies at them and that will be the situation statewide.

We would like to – and Secretary of Public Safety Charles V. Barry has asked me to – encourage our supermarket chains to see if they can't make deliveries to these supermarkets between 10 p.m. and 6 a.m. Then those deliveries can be made and they will not conflict with our snow removal efforts and the other things that are going on during the course of daylight hours.

Post offices will be open and mail can be picked up in person by you, if you want to go down to the post office and pick it up. Some post offices will attempt to make home deliveries again between the hours of 10 at night and 6 in the morning but again, because of the condition of so many of our neighborhoods that have not been plowed out and are still virtually impassable, you should not depend on that.

Eighty-one out of a hundred welfare offices are now open across the state and 13 out of 20 in the Greater Boston area and all 19 Little City Halls in Boston are open to assist people who need public assistance, who may need food stamps, who may need the necessaries of life.

Now, in addition to all of that, banks can open tomorrow (Friday) and also Saturday so long as their personnel can get there on foot or by public transportation. So if you've got to get some money, if you've got to cash a check or withdraw money form the bank, you will have the opportunity to do so in all of those banks and we hope there will be many of them where people can get down by foot or by public transportation.

There are the exceptions or exemptions that will be part of the continued state of emergency.

On the other hand, private passenger vehicles can not and must not be used and the reasons for that again should be obvious to you. We are having increasing problems with people who are running out of fuel oil and need deliveries by fuel oil trucks. We need to get this food, if we can, to our supermarkets. We still have an increasing number of emergency calls and all the rest of it which have to be made. So please do not drive your car, do not use it unless you are essential or emergency personnel. I think everybody knows what that means now.

There is no commercial transportation, no bus or air transportation with the exception of limited service on the MBTA. Logan is closed and will continue to be closed, so far as we know, through tomorrow.

The MBTA has partial service planned for tomorrow. It represents a slight extension of the service that we've had over the past few days.

I've been asked to remind our cities and towns, of course, that schools will not be open tomorrow and I've also been asked to remind all of you to try to conserve fuel as best you can. Not only those of you who are worried about running out but those of you in those areas where there is no state of emergency because to the extent that you use it others may not. So please try to conserve fuel. Keep those thermostats down within reason and see if we can't conserve what we are now some dwindling regional fuel supplies.

Finally, let me say to all of you, that I much appreciate – and all of us do – the continued cooperation of just about everybody. It's important that that continue. I know that some of you are suffering from cabin fever or getting a little stir crazy sitting around in the house. I hope you will just remember that we have some people in this state that barely escaped with their lives; that are sitting homeless and in very, very desperate straits and in churches and in schools, and just think bout them as you wonder about your own problems because you haven't been able to move around.

I guess about the only thing I can suggest is that you go out and take a walk or shovel some more snow, if you haven't had enough of that, or do something – go up to the supermarket. Buy yourself something if you need some food or supplies but please keep those cars in the driveway and the garage. Do not use them and bear with us as we try to continue to make progress – and we are making it – during the course of this next day.

Chapter 4

Blizzard Vignettes: Everyone Has A Story

I t's a fact of life in New England – everyone talks about the weather. It doesn't matter if it's good or bad, hot or cold, rain or shine; there's always something to say about what's going on outside.

Invariably, the discussion will work its way back to the Blizzard of 1978, and each storyteller will try to one-up the other on how they made it through the storm of the century. Some of those are included here, while others are vignettes that might have been forgotten during the past 25 years.

* * * * *

Approximately 350 guests stranded at the St. Regis Hotel in New York City were treated to a taste of the "Manhattan Blizzard" – a drink developed in the hotel bar and poured free for two days.

The drink consisted of the juice of a lime, a teaspoon of sugar and two ounces of light rum blended with a squirt of crème de menthe. This mixture was poured over shaved ice in a champagne glass and garnished with a slice of fresh lime.

Nearly 25 years later, a Rhode Island microbrewery attempted to capture the flavor of the storm with its Newport Storm Blizzard Porter, a beer that is described on its label as "a smooth and drinkable ale designed to keep you warm throughout the winter season."

Coastal Extreme Brewing, based in Newport, says the "winter brew is hand-crafted in honor of the Great Blizzard of 1978" and has a subtle aroma "complimented with crystal and chocolate malts, giving a slightly roasted flavor."

Residents and their faithful companion assess damage along the shore in Nahant. (U.S. Army Corps of Engineers photo)

* * * * *

The Halloween nor'easter of 1991 had no name (unless being called the "No Name Storm" qualifies) until author Sebastian Junger dubbed it "The Perfect Storm" in his 1997 book.

The 1978 snowstorm and flood has been referred to alternately as the "Blizzard of '78" or the "Storm of the Century," but one newspaper in Connecticut gave it a decidedly different name – "Storm Larry."

Sportswriters for The Day, the daily paper in New London, consistently referred to the blizzard as Larry throughout their coverage of high school and college sports cancellations.

For example, the paper reported on Feb. 8 that "Although there were 16 athletic events listed on tonight's Southeastern Connecticut sports schedule, there will be only one winner – Storm Larry, which decimated the entire slate." The next day, sportswriters lamented that "Storm Larry may have gone out to sea, but its effects are lingering as most of Tuesday's athletic contests … have been rescheduled and today's slate is at best 'iffy.'"

There was no explanation given for how Storm Larry got its name, and none of the paper's stories in the news sections used the name to describe the blizzard.

* * * * *

For many Catholics, 1978 will be remembered as the year Ash Wednesday happened on Sunday.

With most churchgoers – and churches – snowed in, Cardinal Humberto Medeiros, Archbishop of Boston, Most Rev. Daniel A. Cronin, Bishop of Fall River, and Most. Rev. Louis E. Gelineau, Bishop of Providence, each postponed the observance of the first day of Lent until the weekend. Each diocese also released Catholics from strict observation of the laws of fasting and abstinence.

Cardinal Medeiros went further, waiving the prohibition on eating meat for the first Friday of Lent, saying that strenuous shoveling of snow required extra nourishment, and that the travel ban had prevented many people from getting to the store to buy fish.

It is believed to have been the first time that Ash Wednesday services were postponed in all three regions.

But not everyone missed out on the blessing and distribution of ashes during the storm. A Catholic deacon from Central Falls was among those stranded at the Rhode Island State House on Ash Wednesday, and held an impromptu service in the building's rotunda. He administered ashes he obtained from nearby St. Patrick's parish to about 130 people at the service, then walked through the rest of the state offices, distributing ashes along the way.

* * * * *

To fight cabin fever, many snowbound New Englanders took to the streets – on foot, of course – searching for something to do. In Boston, the cast of the Broadway musical "Pippin" – the show's opening delayed by the storm – gave impromptu performances at the Park Plaza Hotel. Entertainer Sean Morey, who normally did his juggling, magic and comedy act on Boston Common in warmer temperatures, was a hit at Faneuil Hall and on the Common, where he juggled atop a snowbank. Morey told reporters he was inspired to perform by Gov. Michael Dukakis, who "called me this morning and said, 'This is an emergency. Go out there and make them laugh.'"

Some of those who were stranded away from home in downtown Providence were entertained by the "World's Greatest Disaster Band" on Wednesday evening. Nearly 50 members of the Brown University band marched through the streets of the city, visiting shelters at Union Station, the Civic Center, Holiday Inn and Mathewson Street United Methodist Church.

The band, which had just finished rehearsal for the night, performed its usual playlist, including "Rubber Duckie" and "Up, Up and Away." One man who had been staying at the Civic Center since Monday made a song request – "Show Me the Way to Go Home."

* * * * *

If the blizzard was serious enough to interfere with a holy day like

Lynne Giardino and her brother, Paul, carved this Valentine's Day greeting into the snow outside their Brockton home. (Stanley Bauman photo)

Ash Wednesday, star-crossed lovers had little hope that Valentine's Day could be celebrated without incident the following week.

Flower growers in Massachusetts asked the governor to postpone Valentine's Day from Tuesday, Feb. 14 to Friday, Feb. 17, citing the difficulties in delivering fresh flowers to stores. Many nursery owners suffered crop losses when their greenhouses collapsed under the weight of the snow, leaving them unable to cash in on one of the biggest flower-giving holidays of the year.

Retailers, who feared being left with stockpiles of heart-shaped boxes of candy and leftover cards, pushed for a declaration of Valentine's Week, an idea supported by Providence postmaster Harry Kizirian and the Massachusetts commissioner of food and agriculture. The extension would allow people to get to the store to purchase gifts for loved ones and to make sure that delayed deliveries of Valentine's cards and letters were received.

Boston City Council President Larry DiCara, who had been acting mayor while Kevin White was stranded in Florida, also had lobbied for extending the holiday for a full week, which Dukakis agreed to do.

"It's not the desire of this member of the city council or any other elected official to tamper with matters of the heart," DiCara told reporters. "If Cardinal Medeiros can postpone Ash Wednesday because of the storm, then we can extend Valentine's Day."

Karen Kelly, Kathy Kelly and Lori Anderson use a sled to deliver The Enterprise newspaper on Morse Ave. in Brockton on Thursday, Feb. 9. The girls were filling in for Karen and Kathy's brother, Frank. The travel ban prevented most newspapers from being delivered to newsstands on Tuesday, marking the first time that big dailies like The Boston Globe, The Providence Journal and The Boston Herald didn't reach subscribers. (Stanley Bauman photo)

* * * * *

Schoolteacher Frannie Keyes, who managed the disaster center in Hull, remembers being deluged with calls from anxious residents looking for food, for financial help, or just for information. One of the strangest calls she got was from a woman wanting to know the best way to defrost a waterbed.

If the caller didn't have a clue, the shelter staff wasn't about to make any suggestions.

* * * * *

The snowstorm's traffic troubles played no favorites, as even the chief executives of Connecticut, Massachusetts and Rhode Island were hampered by roads clogged with drifting snow and stalled cars.

Connecticut Gov. Ella T. Grasso left the governor's residence in Hartford at around 3:30 p.m. on Monday, but soon became ensnarled in the nightmarish traffic jam caused by commuters trying to get home. Anxious to get to the state's Civil Preparedness headquarters at the armory,

Army vehicles became common sights on the streets as the National Guard and Army soldiers assisted New Englanders with the cleanup. This Army truck is giving state officials a ride through Providence. (Providence Journal photo)

Grasso ignored the advice of her State Police driver and began walking. Traffic started to move slowly after the governor had covered about a mile on foot, so she hitched a ride with a telephone company worker for the last half-mile to the armory, where she stayed around the clock to supervise the Nutmeg State's emergency relief efforts.

The treacherous driving conditions prevented Massachusetts Gov. Dukakis from traveling to the state's Civil Defense Emergency Operating Center (known as "the bunker") in Framingham, so he set up a command post at the Metropolitan District Commission headquarters at 20 Somerset St., in Boston, near the State House. Dukakis, who usually rode the subway to work, was shuttled between Boston and his home in Brookline by an MDC snow-clearing truck.

Rhode Island's J. Joseph Garrahy, who had struggled for hours to get home to Providence from Newport early Monday, requested help from the National Guard to get to his State House office. At High Service Avenue in North Providence, Garrahy and the Guardsmen encountered a State Police cruiser carrying a woman in labor to the hospital and began pushing abandoned cars out of the way. They even pushed the cruiser until it became stuck in the snow; a passing tow truck then took the woman to Women and Infants' Hospital.

But the governor's troubles were far from over – on the way to the State House, the National Guard truck became stuck near Providence College. While Garrahy was inside getting warm, two dozen students picked up the truck and moved it away from the snow bank. They then hoisted the governor onto their shoulders, carried him outside and sent him on his way.

The truck became stuck again on Davis Street, but Garrahy walked the few blocks to reach his office, which he finally did, four hours after he started the trip, which normally takes about 20 minutes.

* * * * *

In the days following the snowstorm, helicopters crisscrossed the skies as military personnel brought food and supplies to relief workers.

Like castaways on a deserted island, stranded residents carved messages in the snow. Commuters stuck along Route 128 in Massachusetts used their boots to draw arrows pointing to cars that were still occupied. Frustrated residents of Cranston, R.I., sent the message that "This street needs plowing," and in Montville, Conn., residents anticipated that Grasso would take to the skies to survey damage and etched out a 10-foot-tall plea for assistance – "Ella – Help!"

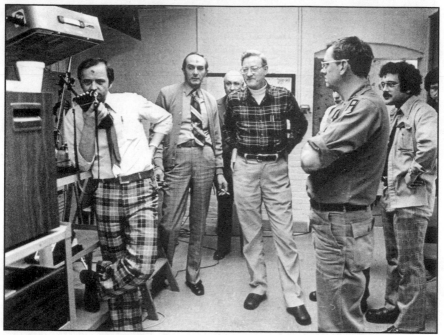

Gov. J. Joseph Garrahy, center, with plaid shirt, supervises relief operations at Civil Defense headquarters at the Rhode Island State House. (Providence Journal photo)

* * * * *

Dukakis wore a sweater over a black turtleneck during the storm; Garrahy wore a flannel shirt.

The governor's fashion statement was still in vogue 20 years later, when he donned the red, white and green plaid for Joe Garrahy's Flannel Shirt Reception, a $100-per-head fund-raiser for the Rhode Island Historical Society.

The event, held at the State House where the governor had commanded the blizzard recovery effort, attracted 100 people who shared their memories of the storm.

Like Dukakis, Garrahy was frequently on TV during the blizzard, and his flannel shirt became so well-known that Rhode Island Sen. John Chafee, prior to a meeting on disaster relief, brought the governor a present.

"After seeing you on television for four days wearing that one plaid shirt, my wife decided you needed a new one," Chafee was quoted as telling the governor.

Garrahy's own family also sent him a change of clothes midweek, along with a small package and a note about what he was missing at home: "Hi, Dad. We miss you. This is a piece of Mom's birthday cake."

* * * * *

Fifty-four deaths were attributed to the Blizzard of 1978, but the other victims of the storm were families trying to plan funeral services for loved ones whose deaths unfortunately coincided with the worst storm of the century.

Faced with driving prohibitions, snowed-in cemeteries and overcrowding at funeral homes, some families were forced to wait days to hold services for the departed. Death notices in Wednesday's edition of The Boston Globe – a paper was printed Tuesday but couldn't be delivered – were dominated by announcements of postponements and time changes for wakes and funerals.

Some Catholic Masses were said in private homes because churches were inaccessible, while other families held abbreviated visiting hours at funeral homes to prevent parking problems and traffic jams.

At one point during the storm, ambulance drivers were unable to get to nursing homes and hospitals to retrieve bodies, and some funeral homes were storing eight to 10 bodies that awaited burial because cemetery roads hadn't been cleared.

"Some rescue people said funeral services should not be considered an emergency," one funeral director complained to Rhode Island's Evening Bulletin. "How would they like to have their mother lying in a morgue for three or four days?"

* * * * *

Lotteries, usually a safe bet as a revenue-generator for state treasuries, suffered millions in losses during the storm. With stores closed, and the driving ban preventing couriers from bringing daily betting slips to Boston, the Massachusetts State Lottery estimated a loss of about $1.8 million in Daily Numbers Game revenues and $600,000 in sales of the weekly Big Money tickets. The storm prevented the drawing on Feb. 8, so the Big Money game was postponed for a week. The Feb. 15 game also was delayed a week, and no tickets were sold for the Feb. 22 drawing so the Lottery could catch up with the calendar.

Rhode Island's lottery commissioners drew numbers for the daily game each night, but also postponed their weekly Grand Lot drawing until the following Wednesday.

One lottery player had to wait more than a week to find out whether he was a big winner. Robert J. Rahill, executive assistant to Rhode Island's governor, purchased a SuperSlot ticket on Monday, Feb. 6. The ticket was a winner, meaning that Rahill could pull the handle on the

Damaged cottages like this one on Newburyport's Plum Island were attractive to looters. The National Guard and local law enforcement kept a vigilant watch for people trying to prey on others' misfortunes. (National Archives and Records Administration photo)

The ocean heaved huge chunks of ice onto the shore at Plum Island, giving the normally tranquil beach an Arctic look. (National Archives and Records Administration photo)

giant slot machine at lottery headquarters in East Providence for a prize. But the lottery would have to wait, as Rahill was in the middle of the state's disaster-recovery effort. He finally was able to get to the lottery office, on Valentine's Day, and with his four children pulling the handle, discovered he'd won the maximum prize — $25,000.

"It looked a lot better to them than snowplows," Lottery Deputy Director Raymond E. Grimes told The Providence Journal.

Twenty years later, the Rhode Island lottery cashed in on storm nostalgia with its "Blizzard of '78" scratch ticket, which offered instant prizes of up to $1,978. Players had to match their winter symbols – scarves, snowshoes, shovels and plows – with the winning symbol in order to win. The colorful tickets included cartoon graphics of snow-covered cars and the familiar symbols for I-95 and I-195, where most commuters abandoned their vehicles in the wind-blown drifts.

* * * * *

There are always those who try to take advantage of a desperate situation. Every corner of the region saw its share of price-gougers and looters – those greedy souls who either marked up the prices of valuable items or simply decided that the blizzard entitled them to take stuff home for free.

Newspapers reported stores doubling the price of a loaf of bread, charging $4 for a half-gallon of milk and hiking the price of a $7 case of beer to $12. The profiteering wasn't limited to businesses, however, as some people purchased the daily papers for 20 cents and resold them on the streets for as much as a dollar. After a Providence supermarket sold out of milk, a woman was seen outside on the sidewalk, trying to sell gallon jugs for $5 apiece.

At the Providence Marriott Inn, the management convinced some of the 2,000 people marooned there to help restock the restaurant by lugging food from a delivery truck stranded on Route 95 – then charged them for the meal!

In addition to forming a human chain to get produce off the highway, people trekked to a local supermarket for milk, bread, beef and orange juice, then walked to a liquor store to restock the hotel bar. When they returned with the provisions, they discovered that prices in the restaurant were discounted only slightly, and the unwilling guests wondered why they "were paying top dollar for food and drink they had carried in on their backs," the Evening Bulletin reported. Hotel managers pointed out that there was plenty of free coffee and fruit avail-

Homes all along the New England shore were devastated by the storm, like the row of cottages on the coast of Maine, above. In the photo below, this home at Camp Ellis, Maine, appears ready to slide down the dune into the water. (National Archives and Records Administration photos)

able in the lobby.

Other scoundrels took a more direct approach, and simply broke into businesses closed or damaged by the elements. In storm-ravaged Scituate, Mass., looters cleaned out the Minot Light Inn's supply of alcohol, including the keg of beer hooked into the bar's tap, but left a bag of pennies in the kitchen. Massachusetts National Guard troops kept watch on summer cottages and waterfront homes in hard-hit coastal areas like Hull, Humarock, Gloucester and Plum Island.

In Quincy, 14 people were arrested for stealing from five businesses; Dedham Police caught four youths stealing $7,000 worth of merchandise from a variety store and sporting goods shop.

Boston Police arrested seven men for breaking into the First National supermarket in Dorchester's Codman Square on Tuesday, then pinched three men at the Cushing Liquor Store on Washington Street. By Thursday, 125 people had been arrested in the city for breaking and entering, with total bail of $12.5 million.

Looters were chased away by police when a tractor-trailer carrying about 4,000 live chickens overturned after crashing into a snowbank at Massachusetts Ave. and Southampton St. According to press accounts, people were carrying away cases of live chickens.

* * * * *

Most kids remember the blizzard as a time they were out of school, but some children spent a good part of the storm stuck *in* school.

In Rhode Island, about 160 students spent two-and-a-half days at the West Warwick Junior-Senior High School, while 450 students and 30 teachers were stuck at the Winman Junior High School in Warwick. The school, located at the top of hill, could not be reached by bus on Monday afternoon, so the elementary students and their teachers had to make the best of it until they were brought home Wednesday afternoon.

Forty-one young students spent several days at the Henry Barnard School, located on the campus of Rhode Island College, including a three-year-old girl whose father became a "guest" after trying to pick her up Monday just as the storm became intense.

In all, about 900 students spent the night at schools in Rhode Island, while several hundred children aboard school buses on their way home had to be rescued; most were reported home by 8:30 p.m. Monday night.

At Mystic Academy in Connecticut, 17 students were forced to stay

Homes that weren't completely destroyed by the ocean were left topsy-turvy when the water subsided, like this house on the southern Maine coast. (National Archives and Records Administration photo)

overnight when their school bus broke down on Monday. The kids took the inconvenience in stride, and even staged their own version of "The Gong Show" to pass the time.

One Warwick student summed up the experience: "It stinks. I would rather be home."

* * * * *

Among the forgotten victims of the storm were animals – pets left behind when people had to evacuate their homes. In Hull, "many persons brought their pets [to the shelters], which added problems," wrote Herb Gordon, editor of The Hull-Nantasket Times. At one point, with 2,000 people crammed into the shelter, town officials considered tranqulizing the animals but reconsidered after lawyers warned about liability for improperly administered drugs.

A family on Sunset Point who evacuated their home because the blackout left them without heat returned to find their fish tank frozen solid.

The dogs and cats who couldn't be brought to shelters weren't completely left in the cold, however, as Gordon pointed out: "The dog

Barbara Smith sits in her father's armchair, the only thing left after her family home on Turner Road in the Sand Hills section of Scituate was destroyed by the ocean. (Kevin Cole/Boston Herald photo)

officer and Animal Rescue League workers began patrols through the floods Tuesday and fed animals left in their homes every day until the emergency ended."

* * * * *

"If you do nothing else, protect yourself with flood insurance and earthquake insurance," a guest speaker recommended at a winter 1977 meeting of community leaders in the seaside town of Hull, Mass.

Earthquakes are relatively rare in Eastern Massachusetts, but floods are commonplace. Although the federal flood insurance program was established in 1968, few coastal property owners had heard of it, and even fewer had purchased a policy. According to studies conducted by the insurance industry, only a fraction of shoreline property owners had adequate flood coverage in 1978; the rest looked for financial help from the federal government's Small Business Administration after disaster struck.

Few people needed a flood-insurance primer more than residents of Hull, a narrow, 2.5-square-mile peninsula that stretches seven miles into Boston Harbor. In the 1960s, the community was forced to construct a massive bayside sea wall after flooding regularly inundated low-lying neighborhoods, and extra-high tides often overwashed roads at critical junctures, turning the town into a series of islands. Some property owners bought flood insurance after a 1972 storm damaged their homes, but only those who obtained mortgages after passage of the Flood Disaster Protection Act of 1973 were required by their lenders to obtain the coverage.

At least one businessman – ironically, a contractor who built sea walls and breakwaters to protect the shore from advancing waves - heeded the speaker's advice and purchased flood insurance that literally saved his assets when the Storm of the Century flooded the New England coastline in February 1978.

He later said he was buying earthquake insurance … just in case.

* * * * *

In Boston, one of the public buildings that became a makeshift shelter was Boston Garden, where the Beanpot college hockey tournament went on as scheduled. In the first semifinal game, Harvard defeated Northeastern in overtime, 4-3. The Boston College-Boston University game was entering the third period when the Garden announcer issued a warning about the storm.

A small cottage community off the coast of Seabrook, N.H. was completely separated from the mainland by flood waters during the storm. (National Archives and Records Administration photo)

He said the roads were impassable, and the last subway train was leaving in 15 minutes; anyone still in the building after that time would likely spend the night there.

Of the 11,666 fans who attended the Beanpot, about 3,000 stayed until the end of the second game, which BU won by a score of 12-5. In all, only 100 or so people remained overnight, including Boston Bruins General Manager Harry Sinden, who slept on a table in a training room.

"An hour after the second game ended, less than 100 were still inside the building," Boston Globe sportswriter Will McDonough reported in Wednesday's paper. "A few went out onto the ice surface, running from one end to the other, sliding headfirst into the nets. A few more huddled around three Harvard band members in the lobby, belting out the Harvard fight song, with two trumpets and a trombone.

"But the rest simply vanished," McDonough wrote. "The same defiance that brought them through the storm was now carrying them home."

Chapter 5

Some Things Will Never Be The Same

The storm of the century had a profound impact on the lives of the people who lived through it, but it also made significant changes on the landscape of New England.

* * * * *

Said to be the most popular subject for painters in the United States, Rockport's "Motif No. 1" was perched at the end of Bearskin Neck for 200 years, but the red fishing shack was no match for the pounding seas of the blizzard.

The trademark of Rockport was crushed by waves on Tuesday and collapsed at about 11:15 a.m., as a group of townspeople watched from across the harbor.

Much of the building was washed out to sea, although a large chunk of the roof remained on the dock. The red shack has been the subject of countless paintings and photographs; artists also sell handcrafted miniature models of the structure, which is frequently featured with fishing buoys lining its side.

In his "Rockport Sketch Book," author John L. Cooley explains how the shack earned its unusual nickname: "America's most-painted building received its name in an impulsive exclamation by Lester Hornby. This illustrator and etcher taught in Paris in the winter; his pupils, in the French manner, drew certain standard subjects or motifs.

"During his summer seasons in Rockport, Hornby noted that many pupils chose the venerable, dilapidated shed on the edge of the inner harbor. Its prominence and its simple but interesting proportions made

Motif No. 1 stood at the end of Bearskin Neck in Rockport Harbor for centuries. A popular subject for artists and photographers, it has been called the most painted building in the world.

The landmark was destroyed during high tide Tuesday morning. It was rebuilt to the exact specifications of the original, and visitors to Rockport today are still greeted by the familiar red fishing shack. (U.S. Army Corps of Engineers photo)

Rockport Harbor, shortly after the storm. The remains of Motif No. 1 can be seen at the bottom center of this view. (National Archives and Records Administration photo)

it a natural model for sketches and paintings, good and bad. One day when a student brought for criticism a pencil drawing of the house, Hornby exclaimed, 'What? Motif No. 1 again?' It has been that ever since."

Owned by the town of Rockport, the landmark was rebuilt to look exactly as it did before the storm. For a brief period, however, the remnants of the old shack attracted the attention of even more artists and photographers, who now were capturing the essence of what was called "Motif No. 2."

* * * * *

As one of the most isolated lighthouses in Maine, Boon Island Light is particularly vulnerable to severe storms. The first two light towers built on the island, about nine miles off York Beach, were washed away by the sea.

When the Blizzard of 1978 roared up the coast, Boon Island was completely submerged. The two Coast Guardsmen on the island retreated to the lighthouse itself, and days later were rescued by helicopter. The keeper's quarters and supply buildings were all destroyed in the storm, and when the ocean receded, the high-water mark was five feet up the tower.

It was no surprise that shortly after the storm, Boon Island Light was automated.

The last manned lighthouse in Maine was on nearby Goat Island, which also was battered by the powerful waves of the blizzard. With part of the island under water, the Coast Guardsman assigned to the light kept watch while his wife and two small children stayed on the second floor of the keeper's quarters. A covered wooden walkway that connected the light tower with the main house was the only casualty of the storm.

Automation appeared likely after the experience during 1978's blizzard, but

Goat Island became a busy place shortly after the 1988 election of President George H. Bush, a summer resident of nearby Walker's Point. The island, which has a commanding view of the Bush home in Kennebunkport, was used as a security station and landing area during the president's term. It was finally automated in 1990.

* * * * *

The heavy surf devastated Cape Cod, wiping out the entire parking

The entire parking lot at Coast Guard Beach in Eastham was washed away by the sea. Officials at the Cape Cod National Seashore became fearful that the bathhouse, which once stood in the middle of the parking area, would float out to sea and burned the building to the ground. (U.S. Army Corps of Engineers photo)

lot at Coast Guard Beach in Eastham and turning Nauset Spit into an island, but for literary types, the real tragedy was the loss of author Henry Beston's Outermost House.

The small cabin, which Beston had named "Fo'castle," was the subject of Beston's account of his time on the Cape's beaches – "The Outermost House," published in 1928.

"Strongly built and sturdy to the end, it quit its foundation posts and floated into the (Nauset) marsh," was how Wallace Bailey of the Audubon Society described the cabin's demise in a letter to Society members on Feb. 9, the same day he identified the bits and pieces of the house that were found at Nauset Heights in Orleans.

One newspaper reported that the author's wife, Elizabeth, said she thought Henry, who died in 1968, would deem the sea reclaiming the cottage "a very suitable end."

Beston had donated the building to the Massachusetts Audubon Society in 1959, and in 1964 the U.S. Department of the Interior declared the tiny cottage a national literary landmark. It was rented to bird-watchers, naturalists and beachgoers each year, among them

Cape Cod's Outermost House, which was the subject of Henry Beston's book by the same name.

Nan Turner Waldron of Sharon, who retraced Beston's activities on the beach and wrote her own book in 1991, "Journey to the Outermost House."

In that volume, she lamented the destruction of the Outermost House, but remained hopeful that Beston's legacy would continue: "In my mind's eye remains the mystery and the wonder of it all," Waldron wrote, "While still the journey lies ahead."

* * * * *

"The storm has united politicians of both parties in mourning the passing of the Good Ship Lollipop, otherwise known as the SS Peter Stuyvesant, site of dozens of political fund-raisers for city and state politicos. The Hudson River cruiser-turned-cocktail-lounge is on its side in Boston Harbor, bearing to the bottom tales of high hopes and political skullduggery," The Boston Globe of Friday, Feb. 10 proclaimed. The paper's Wednesday edition featured a five-column photo of the ship listing to the starboard side in the water next to Anthony's Pier 4 in South Boston, and newspapers everywhere reported on the capsizing of the ship.

Besides its popularity among Pier 4 regulars, the Stuyvesant's story is significant because of the lengths to which owner Anthony Athanas had gone to prevent the former ferryboat from sinking.

A specially designed underwater cradle allowed the boat to rise and fall with the tides, but otherwise held the ship in place. The steel ends of the cradle were attached to 70-foot pipes that were encased in concrete and secured to the bedrock under the restaurant's parking lot.

Athanas purchased the Peter Stuyvesant in 1968 and restored it, fur-

The SS Peter Stuyvesant was used as an excursion steamer on the Hudson River before restaurateur Anthony Athanas brought it to Boston.

nishing the boat with antiques and creating a museum, gift shop and two-story lounge in the interior.

Years later, Athanas was still saying that the Stuyvesant's sinking made him "very sad." In a 1980 interview, the restaurateur said the vessel was insured, but declined to discuss details. He tried several times to refloat and restore the boat but was unsuccessful, and the damaged hull was eventually removed from Boston Harbor.

This structure on a pier in Nahant was another victim of the storm. (National Archives and Records Administration photo)

The amusement area at Salisbury Beach, Mass., was inundated with water when the rough surf pounded the shoreline. (National Archives and Records Administration photo)

What remains of the Five O'Clock Lounge at Salisbury Beach clings to its pilings after being battered by waves. (National Archives and Records Administration photo)

The pounding waves sliced through the Old Orchard Beach amusement pier along the coast of Maine. (National Archives and Records Administration photo)

The world-famous pier at the Old Orchard Beach resort in Maine was heavily damaged, with pieces of the structure among the flotsam and jetsam that washed ashore. A rebuilt pier opened in 1980. (Top: U.S. Army Corps of Engineers photo; Bottom: National Archives and Records Administration photo)

Crews went to work quickly in the aftermath of the storm to shore up the amusement area at Salisbury Beach, which suffered heavy damage to its midway and boardwalk. (U.S. Army Corps of Engineers photos)

A storm of the blizzard's magnitude was sure to cause widespread beach erosion and eat away at cliffs and dunes along the waterfront. These hillside homes near Salisbury Beach have lost much of their back yards to the sea. (U.S. Army Corps of Engineers photo)

The damage at Revere Beach…

(U.S. Army Corps of Engineers photos)

(National Archives and Records Administration photos)

High winds and rough waves did heavy damage at Revere Beach, including tearing the cover off this sun shelter along the waterfront. (National Archives and Records Administration photo)

The oil tanker Global Hope grounded just off Salem during the storm. A pilot boat crew that tried to rescue the men aboard the ship drowned. (U.S. Army Corps of Engineers photo)

Chapter 6

To Hull And Back: Devastation Along The Coast

"Your courage and determination in facing the devastation wrought on this brave community in February, 1978, was an inspiration to all of us in the Commonwealth working to restore normalcy to our shore communities.

"We were proud of the way this community held together and helped the homeless find shelter, the hungry find food and the downhearted find courage and the will to go on.

"Through very desperate days, Hull townspeople and their community leaders held together.

"For centuries to come, proud residents of Hull will look back at the storm of 1978 and remember the splendid and unselfish response of her citizenry in time of need."

— Gov. Michael S. Dukakis, on Hull Appreciation Day

T he first indication I had that we were in real trouble was Monday night," former Hull, Mass. Selectman Myron Klayman remembered, "when I got the call about the water inside Paragon Park."

Klayman, who managed concessions at world-famous amusement park owned by his sister-in-law and her husband, had been in Boston that afternoon with five other local officials to meet with the U.S. Department of Housing and Urban Development. Several times during the ride home along the Southeast Expressway, high winds and drifting snow forced him to pull over and clear off the car.

"We made it home okay," he said. "It was tough, but we did it."

Destruction at Gunrock Beach in Hull…

(National Archives and Records Administration photos)

(National Archives and Records Administration photo)

(U.S. Army Corps of Engineers photo)

Photo taken on Park Ave., just outside Paragon Park, shows the storm's high-water mark in the snow.

But Klayman wasn't prepared for that night's storm update from park caretaker Dillon Kimmery, whose thick Southern accent was unmistakable.

"He called and said, 'Myron, we've got a problem. There's a lot of water here,'" Klayman recalled. Wintertime flooding wasn't unusual at Paragon, which straddled a narrow spit of land between the Atlantic Ocean and Hingham Bay. "I told him to go up to the machine shop. It never floods there. He said, 'I am in the machine shop and I'm in a boat from the Red Mill [the tunnel-of-love ride].' I think he was able to save his lunch, and that was about it."

Later, when Klayman toured the devastated community with the other selectmen, he was amazed by the damage throughout the seaside town, but especially at the 63-year-old amusement park, which had previously survived its share of fires, hurricanes and other natural disasters.

Water had burst through the doors of the video arcade on Nantasket Ave., scattering heavy equipment and fixtures that had been stored for the winter. Outside, the rides had been dismantled at the close of the season, but all of the remaining gearworks and supports were submerged in salt water. Brand-new picnic tables – so heavy that Klayman said they usually took four people to lift – were carried hundreds of yards to the rear of the park and heaved over the fence of the miniature golf course.

The Metropolitan District Commission bathhouse at the foot of Park Ave. on Nantasket Beach was undermined by the rising sea. The building, which dated from the turn of the century, was later torn down and replaced with a concrete-block structure.

"It was incredible, absolutely incredible," he said.

Like Hull, communities up and down the Massachusetts coast suffered water damage that was, as Dukakis declared after a helicopter tour, "awesome."

In Scituate and Brant Rock, shells of houses teetered on weakened supports; other buildings were reduced to piles of rubble. Some homes were completely washed away by the ocean, leaving only concrete foundation walls sticking out of the ground.

Homes that remained standing were missing walls, windows and

Storm scenes from Scituate...

(U.S. Army Corps of Engineers photos)

The surging sea shatters Scituate...

(U.S. Army Corps of Engineers photos)

doors. Some living rooms were filled with rocks, sand and mud, while furniture and personal belongings were tossed mercilessly onto the ground. Sections of roofs that floated away at high tide rested wherever the sea had dropped them.

"I walked down the sea wall at Gunrock, where the majority of homes were torn apart as if some horrid little girl, tiring of her dollies, had kicked in the sides of her doll house to make her point," wrote Tanna Kasperowicz, then a reporter covering Hull for The Patriot Ledger newspaper.

As the storm subsided, the focus of public officials shifted from relief to recovery. President Carter declared eight counties in Massachusetts and the entire state of Rhode Island federal disaster areas, allowing governments to apply for additional cleanup funds.

Disaster centers opened in 14 flooded communities to help residents obtain emergency services and begin the process of rebuilding.

Frannie Keyes, a teacher in the Hull Public Schools, was asked by Dukakis to manage the town's disaster center, which was established at the Damon Elementary School on Atlantic Hill.

"The governor's idea was to have someone local in every disaster center," Keyes said, "so that people would see a familiar face when they got there."

Keyes, who credited schools Superintendent Richard Charlton and residents Larry and Cynthia Kellem with coordinating the town's initial response to the blizzard, said the staff of mostly volunteers provided information on food stamps, medical care, unemployment benefits, flood insurance, reconstruction loans, and crisis counseling.

At the time, Hull was literally and figuratively an island, isolated by flood waters and by National Guard troops, who enforced a curfew and turned away non-residents at the town's borders.

Incredibly, one of the few links to the outside world was the commuter boat at Pemberton, which made its morning run, as scheduled, on Wednesday. With a crew that

Shoulder patch worn by relief workers at the local disaster centers.

Nature's fury engulfs Hull...

The town of Hull was devastated by the elements throughout the storm. Army vehicles removed snow from the front beach area, and also helped rescue families from two homes that burned in Hull Village (middle left photo). The waves were strong enough to flip cars in the Kenberma section and rip apart the boardwalk behind the bathhouse.

(Middle photos from slides by Nazzareno DiVito Jr.; Top and bottom photos courtesy of Barry Haraden.)

now included his entire family, Capt. Norman Rogers shoved off with only one passenger that day, but brought back copies of The Boston Globe for Hullonians looking for the latest news.

With the travel ban prohibiting cars from using the highways, the commuter boat became a transportation system for getting South Shore residents stranded in Boston home from the city. The Nantascot would shuttle them across Boston Harbor to Hull, where they would continue their journey with a National Guard escort.

The driving restrictions in Massachusetts were lifted gradually, and the National Guard's presence in coastal communities ended on Feb. 19. The disaster centers continued operating until March 24, when the two remaining outposts in Hull and Revere were closed by the state. Emergency housing operations, which had involved 62 hotels and 104 private landlords across the state, ceased on April 15.

The long-term effects of the blizzard were addressed through Project Concern, a year-long counseling program that focused on helping residents in the areas hardest hit by the storm - Plymouth, Revere, Scituate, Winthrop, Salem, Hull and Quincy. The emotional scars from the disaster led to alcoholism, suicide attempts and severe depression among some storm victims.

* * * * *

"The Commonwealth emerged from the blizzard because of the extensive efforts of federal, state and local employees and because of the personal contributions and sacrifices of charitable organizations, numerous volunteers, businesses and private citizens," Charles Barry, the Bay State's top public safety official, noted in his final report on the blizzard. "This band of cooperation between the public and private sector extended beyond the actual disaster period."

In storm-ravaged Hull, some residents hadn't yet rebuilt their homes when officials began planning a thank-you party for people who contributed to the disaster-relief effort.

Hull Appreciation Day, co-chaired by Helen Raymond and Barry Haraden, attracted more than 800 people to Hull on July 30, 1978. Beginning with an ecumenical service at Fort Revere, the celebration featured live music, children's games, a dunking booth, free rides at Paragon Park, and a sightseeing tour of the peninsula. Representatives of the Red Cross, the Mennonites, the National Guard, U.S. Army Reserve and the Coast Guard attended the event.

"I probably haven't seen your faces, but I've seen your cellars," local

A grateful community says 'thank you'

Hull Appreciation Day was held on July 30, 1978 to raise money for the organizations that helped the town recover from the blizzard. The day-long event was organized by Barry Haraden and Helen Raymond, and was attended by state and local officials. Shown at the podium are, from left, Gov. Michael Dukakis, state Rep. Mary Jeanette Murray, a representative from Sen. Edward Kennedy's office, Sen. Edward Brooke, and Hull Selectman Myron Klayman. As a fund-raiser, the Appreciation Day

Committee sold souvenir program books with blizzard photos and memories. The committee also sold bumper stickers that featured a slogan, devised by Haraden, that summed up the purpose of the day: 'Thanks a "HULLava" Lot.'

THANKS' A "HULLava' LOT
Survivors - Blizzard of '78

Residents line up outside Hull Town Hall to obtain information about disaster aid.

Red Cross Director George Lamm joked at the Appreciation Day recognition ceremony, which was held on the grounds of the Worrick Mansion on Nantasket Ave.

"On Hull Appreciation Day, it is an honor for me, as governor, to pay my respects to the real heroes and heroines of the disaster recovery – the good and brave people of Hull," Dukakis said. "It is a pleasure to have the opportunity to share this day with you, and to recall your very courageous efforts in the face of the state's worst blizzard in the last 100 years."

The homes along the water's edge on Point Allerton Avenue in Hull also were damaged by the storm. (National Archives and Records Administration photo)

Gunrock home literally wiped off the map...

The photo at top right shows the home at 31 Stoney Beach Rd. in Hull sinking onto Gunrock Beach; the photo at below right is the same house, from the water side. Below, a sandbag sea wall is all that is left to protect homes on Stoney Beach Road; #31 has already collapsed into a pile of rubble. Today, the site has been taken over by the town and is completely empty, with no evidence that a home ever existed there.

(National Archives and Records Administration photo)

(National Archives and Records Administration photo)

The recovery begins...

Houses that were too damaged to be repaired were condemned and razed in the weeks following the blizzard. The views on the next four pages show the cleanup in Gunrock, where buildings were demolished, sea walls were reinforced and debris removed.

(National Archives and Records Administration photos)

(National Archives and Records Administration photo)

(National Archives and Records Administration photos)

(National Archives and Records Administration photo)

The waves undermined the sea wall and boardwalk at Nantasket Beach, leaving an enormous crater in what was once a parking lot. (National Archives and Records Administration photo)

Waterfront roads all over the South Shore were damaged at high tide, including Atlantic Avenue in Cohasset. (National Archives and Records Administration photo)

Even homes with sea walls protecting them were no match for the wind-driven waves. These houses are along Brant Rock in Marshfield. (National Archives and Records Administration photo)

A pier collapsed at Scituate Harbor…

… while part of Glades Road behind the Minot sea wall was washed out. (National Archives and Records Administration photos)

Home at Minot barely clings to the ledge after being destroyed by wind-driven surf. The long, narrow roofline in the right of the photo is the off-kilter house shown at the top of page 116. (National Archives and Records Administration photo)

The powerful sea brought tons of sand, mud and rocks on shore, pushing the debris into houses as waves crashed into them. (National Archives and Records Administration photo)

Some homes were ripped from their foundations in Scituate's Sand Hills section, while others sustained the ocean's attack. This view is near the junction of Turner and Jericho roads. (National Archives and Records Administration photo)

Residents returning to their homes in Scituate not only had to deal with water damage, but some of the streets, such as Turner Road, above, had to be plowed clear of mud and rocks. (National Archives and Records Administration photo)

An Army bulldozer clears a passageway along Third Cliff in Scituate. (National Archives and Records Administration photo)

Homes lost their porches and rear decks when the tides breached the sea wall at Green Harbor in Marshfield. (National Archives and Records Administration photo)

The rising tides left piles of debris behind at the Taylor Street bridge at White Horse Beach in Plymouth. (National Archives and Records Administration photo)

Epilogue

"But, [geologist David Nellis] noted, as little as three months after the storm, 'opinion and pressure have built up so as to permit the rebuilding of just about everything. In fact, the concept today is to proceed with as much speed as possible, and as little input of flood control codes as possible, and to rebuild everything that was destroyed by the storm. Minimal emphasis is being placed on the future safety of the residents in those areas affected by the Blizzard of 1978.'"

— Oceans magazine, Sept. 1978

In the 25 years since the storm of the century battered New England, how many lessons have been learned in regard to emergency preparedness and disaster prevention?

Too few.

During the final editing of this book in early 2003, Congress approved emergency legislation to reauthorize the National Flood Insurance Program, which expired due to lawmakers' failure to act on the issue by Dec. 31, 2002.

For a couple of weeks, the program languished in legal limbo, although federal officials were quick to point out that damage claims filed during the hiatus would be paid. Most policyholders, some of whom incurred losses during an early January coastal storm, had no idea any of this was happening.

What a sad commentary – even members of Congress still don't care enough to take a simple vote on a non-controversial subject before adjourning for the year.

Like the foolhardy souls who didn't heed the storm warnings in 1978, lawmakers are setting the stage for future disasters.

Emergency preparedness also appears to be a low priority for municipalities, even those surrounded by water. Think about it — if you live along the coast, do you know your community's disaster plan? Would you know where to find out?

"Warning systems, evacuation plans and emergency relief programs … are expensive, sometimes inequitable, and piecemeal. Worst of all, they may contribute, as do structural measures, to a false sense of security which may increase the inclination for people to reside in hazardous areas, or to remain there in the face of impending peril," Rutherford H. Platt and George M. McMullen wrote in a 1980 report on post-flood recovery for the Water Resources Research Center at the University of Massachusetts at Amherst.

"Perhaps the most important lesson of the 1978 coastal disaster is that hazard mitigation must be made an integral part of the post-disaster response effort," the report continued. "Our nation must begin to reduce its flood losses as effectively and efficiently as it compensates for them."

Besides ignoring the NFIP's expiration dates, Congress has several flood-insurance proposals lurking in the oblivion of subcommittees. Will any of these bills ever see the light of day? The fact that they have lingered for so long speaks volumes about the unwillingness of lawmakers to address the very basic issue of coastal protection.

Perhaps that unwillingness stems from the fact that disaster-related issues are not at the forefront of the public consciousness – until, of course, we experience the storm of the 21st century.

Boston Globe reporter Michael Kenney, writing in the Sept. 1978 issue of Oceans magazine, summed it up this way:

"For the present, it appears that the absence of strong public support for the acquisition and conservation of the coastline, coupled with the determination of shore property owners to rebuild, have proved stronger than the fury of the February storm. Six months afterward, you bump into someone on a yacht club porch you had not seen since last summer and ask how he had fared in Hull during the storm. 'Hey, not bad,' he replies. 'We've got a new car, a new furnace, most of a new kitchen, and the basement is all done over.'"

Bibliography And Sources

The author conducted numerous interviews with blizzard survivors, relief workers and public officials while researching this book.

In addition, news accounts and descriptions of events were collected from the following newspapers: The Boston Globe, The Boston Evening Globe, The Boston Herald-American, Boston Herald, The Patriot Ledger, The Cape Codder, Cape Cod Times, The Day, The Providence Journal, The Evening Bulletin, The South Middlesex News, Milford Daily News, The Woonsocket Call, Pawtuxet Valley Daily Times, Coventry Townsman, Manchester Union-Leader, Maine Sunday Telegraph, The Hull-Nantasket Times, The South Shore Chronicle, South Shore Mirror, Worcester Telegram & Gazette.

Other sources for this book include:

— "Blizzard of '78: After-Action Report," Commonwealth of Massachusetts Executive Office of Public Safety, 1978
— "Northeast Blizzard of '78: A Report to the Administrator," National Oceanic and Atmospheric Administration, September 1978
— "Blizzard of '78: Coastal Storm Damage Study," New England Division, U.S. Army Corps of Engineers, February 1979
— "Post-Flood Recovery and Hazard Mitigation: Lessons From the Massachusetts Coast," Rutherford H. Platt and George M. McMullen, University of Massachusetts at Amherst, Water Resources Research Center, May 1980
— "The Country Journal New England Weather Book," David Ludlum, Houghton Mifflin Co., 1976
— "New England's Disastrous Weather," Benjamin Watson, Editor, Yankee Books, 1990
— "Coastal Flood of February 7, 1978 in Maine, Massachusetts and New Hampshire," U.S. Geological Survey, U.S. Department of the Interior, 1979

— "Thanks a 'HULLava' Lot: Hull Appreciation Day Program Book," Hull Appreciation Day Committee, July 1978

— "Coming Through," New England Division, U.S. Army Corps of Engineers, February 1978

— "The Economics of Flood Insurance: An Analysis of the National Flood Insurance Program," Gregory A. Vaut, University of Massachusetts at Amherst, Water Resources Research Center, July 1974

— "Dukakis: An American Odyssey," Charles Kenney and Robert L. Turner, Houghton Mifflin Co., Boston, 1988

— "Sea Wall Attack," by Michael Kenney, Oceans magazine, September 1978

— "Answers to Questions About the National Flood Insurance Program," Federal Emergency Management Agency, Washington, D.C., 1992

About The Author

Christopher Haraden has worked as a reporter and editor for various newspapers, including The Hull Times, Banker & Tradesman, Boston Homes and the TAB Newspapers. His publication credits include numerous tourism, historical, financial and real estate publications across New England.

A native of Hull, Haraden serves on the board of trustees of the Fort Revere Park and Preservation Society and is a member of the Hull Historical Society. In 1984, he was the youngest person ever appointed to a municipal board in Massachusetts when he became a member of the Hull Historical Commission at age 13.

In 2001, he was a contributing author for "Hull & Nantasket Beach: Then & Now," a collaborative effort by the Committee for the Preservation of Hull's History. With "Storm of the Century" completed, Haraden will next co-author a revised introduction to the 35th anniversary edition of "Old Nantasket," the classic history of Hull that has been out of print for years. The new edition will be released in the summer of 2003.

He lives in Hanover with his wife, Marilyn, and son, Matthew.

A portion of the proceeds from the
sale of this book will benefit the
Fort Revere Park &
Preservation Society.

Fort Revere Park occupies a site on top of Telegraph Hill in Hull,
Mass. that was a military installation from the Revolutionary
period through World War II. Under the guidance of the non-
profit Fort Revere Park & Preservation Society, the eight-plus acre
site has been progressively cleared, and is now a beautiful hilltop
from which to enjoy the panoramic view of Boston Harbor, and a
charming place to enjoy a picnic.

The site includes a water tower and observation deck, as well as a
growing museum of military history, housed in the fort's former
Officers Quarters on Farina Rd.

Fort Revere Park is open every day from sunrise to sunset, and
offers a variety of recreational and educational opportunities. Event
schedules are posted on the park's Website or are available by
contacting the Metropolitan District Commission, which manages
the site, at the telephone number below.

Donations and volunteers are always needed.

For programming and membership information:
Fort Revere Park & Preservation Society
PO Box 963
Hull, MA 02045
617-727-4468
www.fortreverepark.org

Yes! Please send me my own copy of "Storm of the Century!"

Name_____

Street Address _____

_____

City_____ State _____ ZIP_____

Telephone: _____

E-mail: _____

Send order to:
Times Square Books
30 Aspen Drive
Hanover, MA 02339
781-982-1517

No. of Copies	_____
@ **$19.99** each	
Total	$ _____
MA residents add $.99 tax per copy	_____
Shipping $2.00 per copy	_____
Total due	$ _____

- -

Yes! Please send me my own copy of "Storm of the Century!"

Name_____

Street Address _____

_____

City_____ State _____ ZIP_____

Telephone: _____

E-mail: _____

Send order to:
Times Square Books
30 Aspen Drive
Hanover, MA 02339
781-982-1517

No. of Copies	_____
@ **$19.99** each	
Total	$ _____
MA residents add $.99 tax per copy	_____
Shipping $2.00 per copy	_____
Total due	$ _____